Caring for the Soul:
R'fuat HaNefesh

A Mental Health Resource and Study Guide

Edited by Richard F. Address

UAHC Press
New York, New York

The publisher gratefully acknowledges the following for permission to reprint previously published material:

ABRAMS, JUDITH: Material used in "*Havdalah* Healing Service" adapted from CLAL: The National Jewish Center for Learning and Leadership. Used by permission of Judith Abrams.

BEHRMAN HOUSE, INC.: Excerpt from *Siddur: The Prayerbook* by Ben Zion Bokser. Copyright © 1982 by Behrman House, Inc. Reprinted with permission of Behrman House, Inc.

CENTRAL CONFERENCE OF AMERICAN RABBIS: "Responsa on Disabled Persons," copyright © 2000, CCAR. "Resolution on Caring for Those with Mental Illnesses," copyright © 1997, CCAR. "Responsa on Conversion of a Person Suffering from Mental Illness," copyright © 2000, CCAR. "Responsa on Funeral Service for a Suicide," copyright © 2000, CCAR. "Resolution on Establishing a Complete System of Care for Persons with Mental Illnesses," copyright © 2001, CCAR. Reprinted with permission of CCAR.

HARPERCOLLINS PUBLISHERS INC.: Lines from "Kaddish" from *Collected Poems 1947–1980* by Allen Ginsberg. Reprinted by permission of HarperCollins Publishers Inc.

HYPERION BOOKS: Excerpt from *When Madness Comes Home: Help and Hope for the Children, Siblings, and Partners of the Mentally Ill,* by Victoria Secunda. Copyright © 1977 by Victoria Secunda. Reprinted by permission of Hyperion Books.

PATHWAYS TO PROMISE: Excerpts from "The Bible as a Resource: Materials for Sermons and Articles," edited by Jennifer Shifrin, and excerpts from *Worship Resources* and *How Synagogues Can Help.* Used by permission of Pathways to Promise: Interfaith Ministries and Prolonged Mental Illnesses.

PERLMAN, DEBBIE: "Psalm Two Hundred Forty-Six: The Plague of Darkness," "Psalm Two Hundred Twenty-Three: A Song of Healing for Stella bat Masha," "Psalm One Hundred Seventy-Four: For Seth," "Psalm Eighty-Five: In Iyar: Ani Adonai Rofecha, A Song of Healing," "Psalm Two Hundred Fifty-One: Beginning Therapy," and "Psalm One Hundred Ninety-Nine: Depression." Used by permission of Debbie Perlman.

POLOKOFF, ERIC: Excerpt from *The Shoteh in Formative Rabbinic Literature.* Used by permission of Eric Polokoff.

RECONSTRUCTIONIST PRESS: Adaptation of *"Mi Shebeirach"* from *The Sabbath Prayer Book.* Copyright © 1965, by Jewish Reconstructionist Foundation. Reprinted by permission of Jewish Reconstructionist Foundation.

UNITED SYNAGOGUE REVIEW: "Perfection," by Nancy Blake Lewis. First published in United Synagogue Review, Spring 2001. "Creating Caring Communities: Welcoming the Mentally Ill," edited by Lois Goldrich. First published in United Synagogue Review, Spring 2001. "Everyone Knows Jews Don't Drink . . . And Other Myths About Addiction," by Eric M. Lankin. First published in United Synagogue Review, Spring 2002. Reprinted with permission from the United Synagogue Review.

Contents

Preface

Shalom. This study guide was created as a response to a need, the need to raise awareness of and reduce the stigma within congregations regarding individuals and families who are dealing with mental health issues. These issues reside within every congregation of every denomination. Part of creating a caring and supportive congregation is the need to break down barriers of shame and fear that often are associated with mental health issues. Too many of our people deal with these issues alone, isolated from the spiritual resources that are available to them within their congregational families. Too many congregations hesitate to address mental health issues from the pulpit or within classrooms for fear of raising topics that may make people uncomfortable and may be too difficult. Yet, if our congregations are truly going to be open and inclusive communities, then we need to break down those fears and taboos.

This guide is part of a program being developed by the Union of American Hebrew Congregations. For over a year, the UAHC's Department of Jewish Family Concerns sponsored a series of think tanks and workshops. These sessions were comprised of clergy, mental health professionals, lay leadership, and mental health consumers. The purpose of these sessions was to communicate with people who are familiar with and live with mental health issues on a regular basis. They were asked to consider what an education and awareness program should look like. Their responses led us to conclude that the first step should be the creation of a study guide to be used by lay and professional leadership within a congregation for creating varieties of educational and stigma reduction programs. This guide would be an educationally oriented tool based and framed from within the embrace of sacred Jewish texts.

Caring for the Soul: R'fuat HaNefesh is such a guide. Part 1 focuses on sacred texts that speak to how Judaism began its examination of mental health issues. Part 2 contains traditional and modern Jewish readings of meditations and psalms that can be used in services, support group meetings, educational programs, and the like. Part 3 explores the ways in which Jewish liturgy can address mental illness in our community by providing sample sermons and services. Part 4 discusses the many different types of mental illness, describing symptoms, conditions, causes, and treatment. Part 5 covers the many different ways congregations can put all of this information to use to reach out to the mentally ill and their families. It includes a list of the steps a congregation needs to take to develop congregation-based programs and educational experiences. Sample programs enacted by congregations nationwide are included. Two appendices complete the guide. Appendix A lists additional resources and Appendix B reproduces key mental health related responsa and resolutions recently passed by the Union of American Hebrew Congregations and the Central Conference of American Rabbis.

We hope that the study guide may also be used in dialogues with individuals. As a rabbi, cantor, or educator works with a congregant on issues of mental health, he or she may want to present the guide as a gift from the congregation to the congregant to reinforce the relationship from within sacred texts and tradition. The various prayers, meditations, and psalms should be helpful in these situations.

Caring for the Soul: R'fuat HaNefesh has been created in the hope that congregations, in whatever way they may choose, will begin to think seriously about discussions and programs that will reduce the stigma of mental illness. The goal is *not* to turn every staff person into a therapist or synagogue into a mental health facility. To become a "caring congregation," all manner of issues must be open for discussion within the context of the congregational family. There is a vast reservoir of resources within each of our communities that can be of help in creating caring support for individuals and families who confront the challenges of mental illness.

It should also be mentioned that this guide is by no means representative of every issue. Time, space, and budget do not allow us that luxury. Sections on a wide variety of issues could have been added. We regret that many of the suggestions and some of the materials that were submitted were not included. Hopefully, the material in *Caring for the Soul: R'fuat HaNefesh* will spark discussions and ideas that will lead to programs on many of the issues that are alluded to or were not included. Again, this guide is meant to be a tool to spark such programming and to provide initial ideas and resources that will be developed within congregations.

There are many people who have contributed to the development of this guide. We have attempted to list them in the acknowledgments. Without their input and support, this project would not have evolved. Yet, we must give a special *todah rabbah* to Sari Laufer. Sari is a student at the Hebrew Union College-Jewish Institute of Religion in Los Angeles. During the spring and summer of 2002, Sari collected the voluminous amount of material and notes from the Mental Health Initiative Committee and edited and consolidated this material into a workable document. She also helped edit much of the printed material that was collected, wrote the introductions to the specific sections, and worked to obtain permissions to reprint previously published text. We are all grateful for her dedication, enthusiasm, and commitment to the project.

While *Caring for the Soul: R'fuat HaNefesh* is a product of the Union of American Hebrew Congregations, it is by no means denominationally specific. As you know, the issue of mental health and mental illness encompasses all aspects of the Jewish community. Thus, we trust that the material contained within this guide will be useful in the wide arena of Jewish congregational life.

Finally, it is our hope that your congregation does something to reduce the stigma of mental illness and to raise the awareness of mental health issues within your congregation and your community. Too many of our people feel spiritually alienated from the support of their faith community—support that is seriously needed. Often, as you know, we can heal the soul by our presence and our support. First, we must recognize the need and then not fear to open a door to caring. This is our challenge. May we be strong in creating pathways to meet these challenges from a foundation of faith.

B'shalom,

Rabbi Richard F. Address, D.Min.
Director, Union of American Hebrew Congregations
Department of Jewish Family Concerns
New York, NY 2003

Acknowledgments

Some funding for the development of this study guide was made possible through the generosity of the Alexander Family of Houston, Texas, the Wimmer family of Allentown, Pennsylvania, Temple Sharey Tefilo-Israel of South Orange, New Jersey, and Temple Israel of Minneapolis, Minnesota.

Our appreciation is also extended to the members and regions of the Union of American Hebrew Congregations (UAHC) and the Central Conference of American Rabbis (CCAR) who hosted focused discussions that helped shape *Caring for the Soul: R'fuat HaNefesh*. These include the UAHC Middle Atlantic Council; Rabbi Don Berlin; Temple Beth Ami in Rockville, Maryland; Rabbi Jack Luxemburg; the UAHC Northeast Council; Rabbi David Wolfman; the UAHC Pacific Central West Council; Rabbi Michael Berk; Rabbi Alan Berg; Peninsula Temple Beth-El in San Mateo, California; Rabbi Mark D. Shapiro; and the New England region of the CCAR. Thanks also go to Rabbi Rav Soloff and the Advocates for the Jewish Mentally Ill in Philadelphia, Pennsylvania.

We are grateful for the support of the membership of the UAHC's Department of Jewish Family Concerns, to Chairperson Jean Abarbanel and Vice-chairs Mike Grunebaum and Steve Picheny. The Jewish Family Concerns Mental Health Initiative Committee was headed by Arlene Weintraub of Newton, Massachusetts as well as Dr. Larry Myers and Paula Erdelyi of Louisville, Kentucky. Their committee devoted much time to editing documents and discussing a wide variety of ideas as to the final form of this study guide. Special thanks go as well to Rabbi Ken Lipman and Rabbi Deborah Bronstein for all their help, support, and suggestions; and to Sandy Abramson of Women of Reform Judaism and Dr. Michael Friedman, who assisted in reading through much of the document as it neared completion. We also appreciate the support of the North American Federation of Temple Brotherhoods for providing the insights of John Shalett and Ira Warshawsky.

This project is the work of many dedicated people from the UAHC. We thank Ken Gesser for the support and guidance of the UAHC Press. We acknowledge the assistance and backing of UAHC Vice President Rabbi Dan Freelander and UAHC President Rabbi Eric Yoffie.

Finally, we offer a thank you to Marcia Hochman, assistant director of the Department of Jewish Family Concerns, and Lynn Levy, who directs the UAHC and Jewish Family Concern's premarital project. Both helped to clarify ideas and focus direction for the study guide. Likewise, we thank Anthony Selvitella for his help and Sari Laufer again for all of her dedication, assistance, and caring.

Introduction

Why Do We Need to Be Concerned about Mental Illness?

by Sari Laufer

In the prayer for healing, we ask God to bestow upon the ill a *r'fuah sh'leimah,* a complete, or whole, recovery. We ask not only for a *r'fuat haguf,* a healing of the body, but also for a *r'fuat hanefesh,* a healing of the spirit. For the Rabbis, just as for us today, the mind and the body were inextricably linked; in order to achieve wholeness, both must be healthy.

Talking about physical health has always been a part of life in the Jewish community. From Moses' plea of *El na refa na la* when his sister Miriam became ill, through the American stereotype of the Jewish doctor, physical health and the quest for it has been open and acknowledged. The same is not true of mental health, which has become stigmatized and often ignored in the Jewish community.

Although often ignored, mental illness is far from silent. Millions of Americans are affected daily by mental illness. Approximately 23 percent of Americans and Canadians over the age of eighteen suffer from a diagnosable mental disorder at some time in their lives. Twenty percent of our children—eleven million in all—are afflicted with mental health problems that can be identified and treated successfully. And among our adults over the age of fifty-five, close to 20 percent experience mental disorders that are not a part of the normal aging process. These last two groups—adolescents and older adults—also have high and rising rates of suicide and suicide attempts.

The Jewish community, as in everything else, is not immune. In fact, studies have shown that Jews have one of the highest rates of mood disorders in the country. We all have, or know of, friends or relatives who are affected by this serious and often disabling condition. Yet, despite the prevalence, despite the personal connections, despite the attention given in the larger world, we all too often try to pretend that mental illness does not occur within the Jewish community.

This guide, which is part of an initiative throughout the Reform Movement to raise awareness of mental health issues, is intended to break the silence surrounding mental illness in our communities. From describing the signs of mental illness to listing community and national resources for both the mentally ill and those close to them, we hope to provide clergy and educators with the information they need to be sensitive to and aware of the needs of mentally ill congregants and their families. Aiming for more than simple awareness, we hope that sections on prayer, meditation, and sample sermons will inspire proactive measures to welcome and address those in the community who are affected by mental illnesses.

Mental illness is not a uniquely Jewish problem. But neither is it one that bypasses the Jewish community. And as a community, we must be armed with the tools of knowledge and relevance to give these illnesses uniquely Jewish approaches. If we believe in the power of our prayers for *r'fuat haguf,* it is important that we believe as strongly in the need for and the power of *r'fuat hanefesh.*

In recent years, there has been a plethora of scientific, sociological, and popular written materials addressing the issue of mental illness from a secular point of view. However, these resources do not address our needs and answer our questions specifically as Jews.

Despite our modern beliefs, thoughts, and practices, particularly surrounding medicine and science, we have still been undeniably shaped by millennia of Jewish texts, teachings, and attitudes about the mind, illness, health, wellness, and personality. If we study them carefully, these influences can enhance our more scientific understandings.

The very nature of illness in general makes it a natural concept to address in religious texts and in religious dialogues. Mental illness, even more than other forms of illness, forces us to address and challenge some basic ideas about the world and the ways in which our religion thinks about them. Mental illness forces us to ask such questions as: "Does God play dice with my mental health?" "If God creates the disease, must God also create the healing?" "Can psychiatry/psychology/medicine alone give us the wisdom and the healing we need?"

It would be naïve, in this day and age, to imagine that either medicine or religion alone could provide all the healing and wisdom that we need. But countless studies have proven that a combination of the two can be highly effective in combating illness, both mental and physical.

Our texts provide a natural starting point as we begin to use our religion as a tool in addressing and combating mental illness. "Mental Illness through the Prism of Jewish Texts," a group of excerpts from an essay by Rabbi Kennard Lipman, takes us briefly through various understandings of mental illness in Jewish texts. Beginning with a survey of the understanding of mental health in the Bible, the essay continues with some of the various discussions in Jewish law, which deal with the practical consequences of mental illness in society. Next, the essay briefly touches on the vast body of rabbinic literature that deals with the soul and its moral and spiritual development. In the final section excerpted here, Rabbi Lipman looks at an example of a famous rabbi who both suffered from and taught about mental illness—the Chasidic Rebbe Nachman of Bratzlav.

In addition to providing a uniquely Jewish context from which to address mental illness in our communities, the words of our sacred texts and liturgies can be adapted for new use. In his essay, "Prayer as a Source of Psychological Growth and Well-Being," Rabbi Sanford Seltzer considers the importance of the *Siddur* in history and today, and discusses both avenues to and benefits of forming a connection with the words of the liturgy.

Part I

What Do Jewish Texts Have to Say about Mental Illness?

Mental Illness through the Prism of Jewish Texts

by Rabbi Kennard Lipman

Biblical Literature

Deuteronomy 28 contains a long list of curses that will befall the Israelites if they do not follow the Torah transmitted to Moses. One of these curses makes reference to madness, using a word we all know: *meshugah*. Deuteronomy 28:28 states: "The Lord will strike you with madness *(shigayon),*" while 28:34 declares: "You shall be abused and downtrodden continually until you are driven mad by what your eyes behold." Some scholars have suggested that this indicates two kinds of madness, one coming from God and another owing to circumstances.

But the richest biblical treatment is in the story of David and King Saul: Saul's mental illness is a major part of the story. In 1 Samuel 16:14–23, the prophet Samuel charges David to rule while Saul is still in power:

> Then Samuel took the horn of oil and anointed him [David] in the midst of his brothers, and the spirit of the Lord *[ruach Adonai]* came upon David from that day onwards. . . . But the spirit of the Lord departed from Saul and an evil spirit *[ruach ra'ah]* from the Lord tormented him . . . . And it came to pass, when the evil spirit from God was upon Saul, that David took a lyre and played; so Saul was refreshed and was well and the evil spirit departed from him.

Later (18:13) we are also told, "And Saul was afraid of David because the Lord was with him and had departed from Saul." *Ruach ra'ah*, translated as "evil spirit" does not mean demonic possession; *ruach* means spirit in the sense of wind, breath, or energy.

Ruach, like the English "spirit," denotes a volatile mental state that occupies the whole of a person's consciousness. The Bible speaks of a "spirit of jealousy," but also of a "spirit of knowledge and reverence." *Ruach* may be positive or negative. It may be more or less emotional or cognitive, but it always consists of an upsurge of feeling or energy. Judges 9:23 talks about God sending a *ruach ra'ah* between Avimelech and the men of Shechem. Instead of the metaphor of an "evil wind," we might speak of bad blood between people. The midrash on this passage explains *ruach ra'ah* as *ruach t'zazit,* a perturbing wind, like a squall. This is indeed what it feels like to experience *ruach.* We shall see that the writer William Styron described his depression as a "brainstorm" and lamented that this metaphor has taken on an almost exclusively positive sense. Another ancient midrash confirms this meaning when it says: "When a person has *ruach ra'ah* then all his words and thoughts come from it." The Mishnah (the earliest text of Jewish law) says that a person who extinguishes a Shabbat candle because of *ruach ra'ah* cannot be held responsible for violation of the law.

To return to the story of King Saul: scholars have speculated as to the nature of his illness. Did he suffer from paranoid schizophrenia or perhaps a bipolar (manic depressive) illness? The Bible is not, however, biography and history in the modern sense. Scholars continue to debate the historical value of the Bible. It may not give us historical information about the man Saul, but at least it gives us a glimpse of what the attitudes of the authors/compilers of the text were toward mental illness. What does the text tell us about the biblical understanding of mental illness?

The verses quoted above seem to indicate that Saul's illness is connected to his and David's intense rivalry. But, as in the case of Deuteronomy 28:28, why should the Bible insist that the illness comes directly from God? Furthermore, why should music have had the power to heal, or at least to alleviate, such illness?

It was understood in the ancient world that music had the power to induce states of religious ecstasy and prophecy. This brings us to another important aspect of the biblical understanding of mental illness. *Ruach* could also designate states of prophetic inspiration. In order to understand why *ruach* and prophecy should be so closely connected, we need to realize that in the biblical period, prophecy was as much an institution as a state of religious ecstasy. Practical and legal decisions were made on the basis of prophecy. Saul tried to combine the roles of both king and prophet. 1 Samuel 18:10–13 says: "An evil spirit from God *[ruach Elohim ra'ah]* came upon Saul and he raved in the midst of the house." He then tried to kill David. The word translated as raved is *yitnebei,* literally, prophesied (a *navi* is a prophet). The Bible saw a connection between madness and prophecy; this is also evident in the story of the prophet Ezekiel, who also exhibited bizarre behavior. Prophets sometimes traveled in groups, practicing methods for inducing prophecy by music and other means. Verses 19:23–24 also make this association, where we are informed that Saul had prophetic powers:

> And the spirit of God was upon him [Saul] also and he went on, prophesying . . . and he even stripped off his clothes and he himself prophesied before Samuel and lay down naked all that day and night. Therefore, they say, "Is Saul also one of the prophets?"

Shortly after this incident, 21:14–16 describes David feigning madness to escape from Akhish, King of Gat, after fleeing from Saul. The verb for "acting mad," *yitholeil,* comes from the root *h.l.l.,* "cry aloud; praise" (as in *hallel*), once again indicating the association of madness with ecstatic behavior of a religious kind.

Numbers 11:28 describes how Joshua urged Moses to put a stop to the spontaneous prophetic outbursts that were occurring in the Israelite camp in the desert. The great commentator, Nachmanides, says that Joshua was worried that a *ruach ra'ah* or a *ruach sheker,* a spirit of falseness, would overcome them; in other words, they would become false prophets and lead the people astray.

In short, the biblical writers and commentators were acute observers: they saw that *ruach* indeed possessed a person, like someone caught up in a storm, but they had broken with the ancient pagan notion that this meant possession by a malevolent or benevolent entity.

Rabbinic Literature

The Talmud and later Jewish law discuss mental illness in two principal areas: (1) determining whether an individual is competent to act as a legal agent—*shoteh;* and (2) determining whether there is a threat to one's own or to another life—*sakanat nefashot.*

Shoteh means someone who is incompetent to act as a legal agent in civil cases (such as testifying in court or being liable for damages) or religious matters (such as fulfilling mitzvot). It is used to refer both to the mentally ill and to the developmentally disabled. It was only in the nineteenth century that this stigma of incompetence was removed from the deaf and the mute *(cheresh),* when their normal intelligence was demonstrated to rabbis.

The Talmud and legal codes such as Maimonides' *Mishneh Torah* contain fascinating discussions as to how to determine whether one is a *shoteh* in the sense of mental illness. The Talmud takes a primarily behavioral approach: What actions qualify a person as mentally ill? Do actions such as tearing one's clothes, sleeping in a cemetery, or destroying what is given to the person constitute *shoteh?* Shall we make a list of such behaviors and determine that a person is *shoteh* when he or she exhibits one of them or a certain minimum number of them (as is still done today in diagnosing depression, for example)? Maimonides took the discussion a step further by going beyond the behavioral approach and asking about the mental state of the person: Has he or she lost his or her rationality or not?

Several terms are used in this discussion to refer to mental illness. Probably the most well-known is *marah shechorah,* black bile, which is the literal meaning of melancholy, which we today would call a form of depression. *Teiruf daat,* literally a tearing of one's mental state, indicates a temporary state of mental distress that could render one *shoteh* or could be a threat to one's health and safety. According to one authority, *teiruf daat* could "range from gross psychological decompensation to forms of psychosocial anguish" (Moshe H. Spero, *Handbook of Psychotherapy and Jewish Ethics,* 21).

The issue of threat to life *(sakanot nefesh)* is an important one. Jewish law clearly recognized that mental illness could be a threat to life. Halachah could be violated in order to save life *(pikuach nefesh),* such as preparing medicine on Shabbat or eating a nonkosher food for health reasons. Mental illness was treated like physical illness. Of particular interest to us today is that in matters of abortion and contraception, the Rabbis permitted them when not only the woman's physical health was in danger, but her mental health as well. The Rabbis even affirmed the validity of saying the prayer upon recovery from illness *(Birkat HaGomel),* upon the recovery from mental illness or even upon significant alleviation of symptoms where there is no definitive cure. One congregant made a profound observation when she returned to congregational life after a bout with severe depression: "I never understood, nor could I say, the traditional form of the second blessing of the *Amidah,* 'who gives life to the dead,' until I recovered from severe depression."

Ethical Literature

Rabbinic ethical literature spans two thousand years, from *Pirkei Avot (Sayings of the Fathers)* in the Mishnah, to the latest in spiritual advice from contemporary rabbis. One of the most famous examples of rabbinic ethical literature is Maimonides' *Eight Chapters (Shemonah Perakim: A Treatise on the Soul,* translated by Rabbi Leonard Kravitz and Rabbi Kerry Olitsky and published by the UAHC Press), which discusses the sicknesses of the soul and how to cure them. While Maimonides was influenced by the ethical and soul theories of Aristotle, he is part of the mainstream of rabbinic ethical theory, what philosophers today would call a virtue *(midot)* theory of ethics. In other words, in answer to the question "How do you become a good person?" the Jewish approach has been to develop, through thought and action, positive qualities in imitation of God's qualities of love, awe, justice, and so on. Maimonides said:

> The ancients said that just as health and sickness applied to the body, so health and sickness applied to the soul. The soul is healthy when every aspect produces good and every action is fitting; the soul is sick when every aspect produces evil and every action is reprehensible. Virtues are those elements of character midway between two qualities that are bad: one excessive and the other absent. From virtues come good acts. Prudence, for example, is midway between excessive desire and its absence. Generosity is midway between miserliness and extravagance. Humility is midway between pride and shame.... Should one's soul be ill, one should proceed in the same manner as one would proceed in the treatment of ills of the body. If the body loses its harmony and moves to one extreme or another, then one moves to reverse the process.

While such ethical teachings show great psychological insight into the issues with which we normally wrestle, the problem with such traditional teachings about the soul and the advice they give is that they do not distinguish between transitory, nonclinical depression and mental illness. Some rabbis have tried to combine such traditional ethical teachings with contemporary psychological insights. For example, Rabbis Byron Sherwin and Seymour Cohen, in a chapter entitled "How to Deal with the Ego" in their book *How to Be a Jew,* state:

> Anger channeled inward at the self manifests itself as depression. Long after psychologists such as Heinz Kohut identified pride and depression as complementary aspects of narcissism, Hasidic teachings described depression as the flip side of pride. In the Hasidic parlance, depression, like pride, is a form of idolatry in that egocentrism replaces God as the object of ultimate concern. It places one's momentary unfulfilled needs and desires at the center of one's concerns. In this regard the Baal Shem Tov taught, "The main rule in serving God is that you should keep yourself far from sadness and depression to the very best of your ability." (84)

While this might be good advice for many of us, it does not distinguish between the normal, deep sadness we might experience in the course of life and "major" or "dysthymic" depression, or even between normal, deep sadness and "adjustment disorder with depressed mood," a transient form of depression. Telling the clinically depressed person that "depression is a form of idolatry" will clearly not be helpful.

But does this mean that mental illness is totally outside the realm of ethics? Maimonides in his *Hilchot T'shuvah (Laws of Repentance)* gives the basic Jewish position on free will: We are free to choose between the bad and the good. God or astrology or genetics do not determine how we will act ethically. The choice is ours. However, there is a seeming contradiction to free will in the Torah: God hardens Pharaoh's heart so that he will not let our people go. Maimonides and other Rabbis explained this contradiction as a metaphor for how evil choices lead the evildoer into more evil, to the point where he or she is so enmeshed in the evil deeds that it is very difficult to change. In the case of mental illness we could ask, Does the schizophrenic have free will?

A very moving answer in the affirmative is given in the following story about a schizophrenic brother in Victoria Secunda's *When Madness Comes Home: Help and Hope for the Children, Siblings, and Partners of the Mentally Ill:*

> I guess I just snapped, because nothing I did made any difference. I said to [my schizophrenic brother], "That's it. You're on your own. You can figure out how to get your Social Security payments, where to live, how to make bail. I am finished with you." Well, within twenty-four hours he got himself into treatment. He's living in a halfway house where he follows the rules. He's no longer violent. He's clean and takes his meds. Mentally ill people are capable of some volition, some rational thinking. I can't tell you how much better I feel about him. I really look forward to seeing him now, because he's helping himself. (269)

We have a similar testimony from Peter Whybrow, a psychiatrist who specializes in mood disorders. In his book *A Mood Apart: Depression, Mania, and Other Afflictions of the Self,* he says, on meeting a patient in the midst of a postpartum psychosis:

> But even in madness a vestige of the normal self remains, observing amidst the turmoil, and it is to this fugitive of objective reason that one must address oneself. "Hello, Mrs. Branch," I said, holding out my hand in greeting. "My name is Dr. Whybrow." For somebody as disturbed in thought as Melanie was that early morning, these simple words are not frivolous details, as one may think, but important acts of caring. Even in madness we are each entitled to civility and an honest introduction from those who offer their healing prescriptions. (203–4)

Rabbi Nachman of Bratzlav

> "All the illnesses people suffer come only because of a lack of joy."
> —*Likutei Moharan (Writings of Rabbi Nachman),* II, 24

Rabbi Nachman (1772–1810) was one of the most famous of all Chasidic masters. His followers today, the Bratzlav Chasidim, make up the second most influential Chasidic group in the world, after the Chabad Chasidim. While it might be very difficult to determine whether a biblical figure was mentally ill, in the case of Rabbi Nachman we have biographical materials, as well as his own writings, that indicate that he might have suffered from bipolar (manic depressive) illness. Rabbi Arthur Green, in his definitive biography of

Nachman, *Tormented Master,* quotes from the writings of his principle disciple, Rabbi Nathan, who wrote about his teacher as follows:

> No act in the service of God came easily to him; everything came only as a result of great and oft-repeated struggle. He rose and fell thousands and thousands of times, really beyond all counting. . . . He would enter into worship for a certain number of days; then again he would experience a fall. . . . It was his way to start anew each time. . . . At times he had several such new starts within one day, for even within a single day he could fall several times and have to begin all over again.

Rabbi Green also notes that mental illness can reflect the society in which the sufferer is a part, often in very profound ways:

> Erik Erikson's *Young Man Luther* [a psychological portrait of the Protestant reformer by the well-known psychoanalyst] is claimed to be of particular significance because it was the story of a personality who, more than any other, embodied within himself the struggles and crises of his age. . . . Nachman is precisely such a figure. The central issue of his religious life, his constant awareness of the absence of God from the ordinary universe of human experience, still unique for a Hasidic master, was to become dominant in the lives of generations of Jews who came after him. . . . His struggle, at some points with guilt and thus with his own unworthiness to evoke the presence of God, at other times with doubt, or the absence of God from those lives and moments that did seemingly merit His attention, remains a *single* struggle. . . . Nachman not only was a figure who personified the crisis of this age . . . but also, unlike Luther, *was conscious* of his role as such a figure . . . the suffering *tzaddik* [righteous teacher]. . . .

Rabbi Nachman's mental illness does not detract from his accomplishment. Knowledge of it should enhance our appreciation of what he had to overcome. Despite his disability he was able to teach and inspire thousands of Jews in his day and countless more since then. One of his sayings, "Jews, do not despair!" was written in Yiddish, "*Gewalt Yiden, zeit sich nit meyaesh,*" over the entrance to the Breslov *shteibel* in the Warsaw Ghetto. There is hardly a synagogue-going Jew in America today who doesn't know a tune for his "Kol HaOlam Kula Gesher Tzar Me'od" (All the world is a narrow bridge, [the important point is not to fear at all]).

Prayer as a Source
of Psychological Growth
and Well-Being

by Rabbi Sanford Seltzer

Long before the emergence of psychological schools of thought and the advent of the practice of psychotherapy as an avenue for problem solving and achieving mental health, Jews turned to prayer for guidance, comfort, wisdom, and inspiration. Within the pages of the prayer book, they found the strength to face the stresses of daily life and the faith to persevere despite both personal and collective misfortunes. The historic importance of the prayer book or *siddur* in Jewish life is captured most beautifully in the words of Harry Slonimsky: "I regard our old Jewish Siddur as the most important single Jewish book, a far more personal expression, a closer record of Jewish suffering, Jewish hope and aspiration than the Bible. . . . The Jewish soul is mirrored there as nowhere else."[1]

For the contemporary Jew, prayer has been more of a problem than a solution. Its value as a potential source of growth and well-being is seldom considered. Many would doubt its capacity to provide the pathways to meaning and fulfillment that our forebears derived from it. Consequently, much effort continues to be expended in prayer book revision in the hope that revisions will bring about a deeper appreciation of its contents, a greater devotion to prayer, and an increase in synagogue attendance. Certainly prayer books have changed repeatedly as the Jewish experience has changed. Revising them is a long and honorable tradition in Judaism although it bears mentioning that the basic rubrics of the service have essentially remained the same.

But a good part of the dilemma over the so-called irrelevance of prayer in our day may lie not in rewriting texts, but in the failure or inability of the worshipper to ponder more deeply the message they bring. It is not incidental that the word liturgy is derived from the Greek, meaning the work of the people. For prayer to be purposeful, the worshipper must be open to the possibilities it conveys and not enter the experience with a mind and a heart that are already closed. Psychotherapists use the terms resistance and denial to describe those

---

[1]Harry Slonimsky, *Essays* (Cincinnati: Hebrew Union College Press; Chicago: Quadrangle Books, 1967), 120.

mechanisms by which some clients avoid confronting themselves and the underlying issues that brought them to the therapist's office in the first place.

It is not uncommon for such people to abandon the therapeutic process entirely, insisting that the cost is too high, the treatment is too lengthy, or the clinician is ineffective in helping them cope with their problems. While sometimes these complaints are valid, they are often indicative both of a reluctance to continue and the need to find a rationale for stopping prematurely.

Similar mechanisms of defense can be applied to the mindset of many Jews as they approach prayer and the prayer book. If one is unwilling to engage in the prayer experience, or does so with hostility or ambivalence, no amount of prayer book revision will matter. This is not to suggest that prayer should be construed as a substitute or an alternative if or when psychotherapy is necessary. It is to suggest that the insights gained from prayer are not only intrinsically rewarding, but may be beneficial for those who though troubled have been fearful of seeking professional help. Having opened themselves to prayer, they may now be more prone to reconsider their fears.

It is significant that the word for prayer in Hebrew, *t'filah,* and the verb form "to pray," *lhitpalel,* connote efforts at intervention and even argument on the part of the worshipper. The act of prayer implies a form of self-evaluation. It presupposes an attempt to assess oneself and one's identity. It points to a readiness for probing beneath the superficial. It is a starting point for deeper introspection.

A closer look at just a few of the prayers in the daily morning service known as *Shacharit* are illustrative of how prayer can contribute to the worshipper's self-awareness. The very structure of the service is a tribute to the insights of the rabbis who edited the first compilations of the prayer book centuries ago and who were amazingly attuned to the individual's underlying concerns and aspirations. Most of these compilations are still found in our prayer book, albeit in modified form.

The word *Shacharit* itself is noteworthy. Tradition attributes its origins to Abraham, just as the afternoon and evening services are assigned to Isaac and Jacob respectively. We are told in Genesis 19:27 that Abraham "got up early in the morning in the place where he had stood before the Eternal." The rabbis interpret the verse to mean that upon awakening, Abraham's first act was to pray to God.

Shacharit comes from the root "to free," or "to open up." To label the service of worship with which one greets the new day as an occasion for inner growth is a profound concept. To be told that daily we are given another chance to avail ourselves of the possibilities inherent in the world around us is a remarkable declaration. To be informed that the potential for intellectual and emotional release is constant if only we are willing to accept the challenges that these present is very powerful. To know that the very description of that moment in time set aside for meditation and self-searching creates its own expectations can be both exhilarating and demanding.

A case in point is the prayer that one is to recite following a night of sleep that has hopefully brought rest and refreshment to one's body and spirit. "Modeh ani Lfoneho Melech chai Vkayom. Shehehezarto bi Nishmati Bhemlo, Rabah Emunateho. I thank you Eternal God who has restored my soul to me. How great is your faithfulness."[2] Immediately upon rising, one expresses appreciation and wonderment at being accorded another day of life.

---

[2]Philip Birnbaum, *HaSiddur HaShalem: The Daily Prayer Book* (New York: Hebrew Publishing Company, 1949), 1.

One acknowledges his or her worth as a person and with all humility the miraculous phenomenon of breathing. The day starts with a heightened feeling of self-esteem. Moreover, the Hebrew word *emunah*, or "faith," is derived from a root that can also denote an artistic creation. What can be more marvelous than to behold oneself as special, as creative achievement?

Martin Buber cites the words of the Maggid of Zlathcov: "It is the duty of every person in Israel to know and consider that he is unique in the world in his particular character and that there has never been anyone like him in the world."[3] What a contrast to being prone, as we generally are, to take life for granted, rarely pausing to reflect upon the grandeur of either our physical attributes or our mental faculties. It is only when we become ill or impaired that the full enormity of what once was ours, and the magnitude of our loss, become apparent to us.

Abraham Joshua Heschel called them "the miracles that are daily with us." He understood them to be another reason for prayer. "There is," he wrote, "no worship, no music, no love, if we take for granted the blessings and defeats of living. No routine of the social, physical, or physiological order must dull our sense of surprise at the fact that there is a social, physical, or physiological order."[4]

The prayer book reminds the worshipper to recognize these gifts and to internalize their significance by proclaiming each morning: "Blessed is our Eternal God, creator of the universe, who has made our bodies with wisdom, combining veins, arteries, and vital organs into a finely balanced network. Wondrous fashioner and sustainer of life, source of our health and our strength, we give you thanks and praise."[5]

There is here an expression of gratitude and of awe. Moreover, by confirming the harmonious interaction of the organs of the human body, one commits oneself to their maintenance and care as well. The prayer and blessing with which this proclamation concludes speak to the transcendent dimension of the human condition.

The Hebrew word for blessing, *brocho,* refers literally to the knee. We bow to a higher source of authority. We convey our intention not to squander these treasures but to nurture them with proper diet, exercise, and mental stimulation, and to avoid or minimize behaviors that are self-destructive. We affirm that each of us is part of a greater community and that in safeguarding our own health and welfare we contribute to that of others.

But what of those who have not been so endowed and who, through no fault of their own, suffer from an incurable illness or a congenital infirmity? For them there can be no more profound truth than the recognition of the delicate balance that must prevail if the constituent parts of the human body are to function smoothly. As they "praise the wondrous fashioner and sustainer of life," they voice their faith and their determination to be undismayed by their deprivation and to go forward with their lives.

It is not incidental that in the choreography of the prayer book, what follows this articulation of wonder at our very being are the guidelines that Judaism has established for living a wholesome and productive life, and by so doing contributing to the betterment of society: "These are the obligations without measure, whose reward too is without measure. To honor mother and father, to perform acts of love and kindness, to attend the house of study daily. To welcome the stranger, to visit the sick, to rejoice with the bride and groom,

---

[3]Martin Buber, *Hassidim and Modern Man,* ed. and trans. Martin Friedman (New York: Horizon Press, 1958), 140.
[4]Abraham Joshua Heschel, *God in Search of Man* (Philadelphia: Jewish Publication Society, 1959), 49.
[5]*Gates of Prayer: The New Union Prayerbook* (New York: Central Conference of American Rabbis, 1975), 51.

to console the bereaved, to pray with sincerity, to make peace where there is strife. The study of Torah is equal to them all, because it leads to them all."[6]

There is a prophetic, almost messianic dimension to their being couched as incumbent responsibilities rather than items of choice. The phraseology is deliberate. It defines the criteria for adult maturity. Through the performance of these deeds, building a caring community from which everyone benefits is realizable. In rejecting them, by living selfishly and egocentrically, that prospect is jeopardized. Immediately following these pronouncements the worshipper is called upon to accept one of the foundational principles of Judaism, one that can be described in psychological language as an exercise in sound reality testing and healthy ego reinforcement: "The soul that you have given me, O God, is pure. You have created it and formed it, breathed it into me and from within me you sustain it. So long as I have breath therefore, I will give thanks to you O Lord my God and God of all ages. Blessed is the Lord, in whose hands are the souls of all the living and the spirits of all flesh."[7]

The prayer envisions a holistic view of life. It asserts the decency and innocence of every human being at birth. Guilt and self-reproach are not to be understood as inherent in the human condition, but as the result of voluntary, intentional actions. We are reminded that because life is transitory and its end is beyond mortal control, it is all the more precious and fragile. Death's inevitability is a challenge to live life to the fullest.

There is then an abiding truth to Slonimsky's characterization of the *siddur* as the heart and soul of the Jewish people. The prayer book can be a vital resource for modern Jews as it was for our people in past generations. With this in mind, the words of Moses in Deuteronomy 30:11–14 are most fitting: "Surely this instruction which I enjoin you this day is not too baffling for you, nor is it beyond reach. . . . For this thing is very close to you in your mouth and in your heart to observe it."

---

[6]Ibid., 52.
[7]Ibid., 53.

Part 2

Whence Will Come Our Aid?

Jewish Readings of Comfort and Encouragement

Throughout our history, our sacred texts have been a source of solace in times of personal and communal suffering. "Textual Sources for Meditation or Thought," contains relevant biblical passages annotated with regard to mental illness. "Traditional Psalms" and "Modern Psalms" offer incredible words of comfort and guidance in times of need.

Textual Sources for Meditation or Thought*

And God created man in His image, in the image of God He created him;
male and female He created them.

—Gen. 1:27

This crucial line reminds us that all of us—male, female, healthy, and ill—are created b'tzelem Elohim and are therefore deserving of equal treatment.

The spirit of the LORD God is upon me, because the LORD has anointed me to bring good tidings to the afflicted; He has sent me to bind up the brokenhearted, to proclaim liberty to the captives, and the opening of the prison to those who are bound.

–Isa. 61:1

The LORD sets prisoners free; the LORD restores sight to the blind;
The LORD makes those who are bent stand straight; the LORD loves the righteous;
The LORD watches over the stranger; He gives courage to the orphan and the widow.

—Ps. 146:7–9

He shall not decide by what his eyes behold, nor decide by what his ears perceive. Thus shall he judge the poor with equity and decide with justice for the lowly of the land.

—Isa. 11:3–4

In the eyes of God, the weak and the infirm are treated equally with the strong and the healthy. Thus, within our communities, we must strive to do the same thing. Reform Jews have always taken seriously

---

*Pathways to Promise is an interfaith technical assistance and resource center that offers liturgical and educational materials, program models, and networking information to promote a caring ministry for people with mental illness and their families. Many of the following passages, along with the explanations, were adapted from their brochure: "The Bible as a Resource: Materials for Sermons and Articles," edited by Jennifer Shifrin. She has taken selections from throughout the *Tanakh,* many of which focus on treatment of the weak and the oppressed—the widow, the orphan, and the stranger among us. Included here is just a sampling of such passages. In some cases, we have included possible tie-ins to the issue of mental illness in the community.

our commitment to stand up for those who cannot stand up for themselves. We must always remember to include the mentally ill within our community.

Protect most carefully your souls . . .

—Deut. 4:15

In distress I called on the LORD; the Lord answered me and brought me relief.
                    —Ps. 118:5 (also part of the Hallel service)

My tears have been my food day and night; I am ever taunted with "Where is your God?"
When I think of this, I pour out my soul:
How I walked with the crowd, moved with them, the festive throng, to the House of God with joyous shouts of praise.
Why so downcast, my soul, why disquieted within me?
Have hope in God; I will yet praise Him for His saving presence.

—Ps. 42:4–6

Traditional Psalms

Throughout the generations of Jewish history, *t'hillim* have been recited in times of trouble. Sources as far back as Rambam, in his *Hilchot Avodat Kochavim,* touched upon the idea of reciting *t'hillim* for protection from harm. Today, we are familiar with the recitation of Psalm 23 ("The Lord is my shepherd, I shall not want") in a house of mourning, or Psalm 150 as part of the daily and Shabbat morning worship services, but all too often other psalms are overlooked.

Here, you will find excerpts of psalms commonly used in healing services and prayer circles. All translations are from the Jewish Publication Society's *Tanakh.*

Psalm 27
Verses 1–5

The LORD is my light and my help; whom should I fear?
The LORD is the stronghold of my life, whom should I dread?
When evil men assail me to devour my flesh—
    it is they, my foes and my enemies, who stumble and fall.
Should an army besiege me, my heart would have no fear;
    should war beset me, still would I be confident.

One thing I ask of the LORD, only that do I seek;
    to live in the house of the LORD all the days of my life,
    to gaze upon the beauty of the LORD, to frequent His temple.
He will shelter me in His pavilion on an evil day,
    grant me the protection of His tent,
    raise me high upon a rock.

Psalm 30
Verses 2–12

I extol you, O LORD, for You have lifted me up,
    and not let my enemies rejoice over me.
O LORD, my God, I cried out to you and You healed me.
O LORD, You brought me up from Sheol,
    preserved me from going down into the Pit.

O you faithful of the LORD, sing to Him,
    and praise His holy name.
For He is angry but a moment, and when He is pleased there is life.
One may lie down weeping at nightfall; but at dawn there are shouts of joy.

When I was untroubled, I thought, "I shall never be shaken,"
    for You, O LORD, when You were pleased,
      made [me] firm as a mighty mountain.
When You hid Your face, I was terrified.
I called to you, O LORD; to my LORD I made appeal,
    "What is to be gained from my death, from my descent into the Pit?
Can dust praise you? Can it declare Your faithfulness?
Hear, O LORD, and have mercy on me; O LORD be my help!"

You turned my lament into dancing,
    you undid my sackcloth and girded me with joy,
    that [my] whole being might sing hymns to You endlessly;
    O LORD my God, I will praise You forever.

Psalm 42

Verses 2–6

Like a hind crying for water, my soul cries for You, O God;
    my soul thirsts for God, the living God;
    O when will I come to appear before God!
My tears have been my food day and night;
    I am ever taunted with, "Where is your God?"
When I think of this, I pour out my soul:
    how I walked with the crowd, moved with them,
      the festive throng, to the House of God with joyous shouts of praise.
Why so downcast, my soul, why disquieted within me?
Have hope in God; I will yet praise Him for His saving presence.

Psalm 77

Verses 2–10

I cry aloud to God; I cry to God that He may give ear to me.
In my time of distress I turn to the Lord, with my hand [uplifted];
    [my eyes] flow all night without respite; I will not be comforted.
I call God to mind, I moan, I complain, my spirit fails. *Selah*.

You have held my eyelids open;
    I am overwrought, I cannot speak.
My thoughts turn to days of old, to years long past.
I recall at night their jibes at me;
    I commune with myself; my spirit inquires,
      "Will the Lord reject forever and never again show favor?
Has His faithfulness disappeared forever?

Will His promise be unfulfilled for all time?
Has God forgotten how to pity?
Has He in anger stifled His compassion?" *Selah.*

Psalm 88
Verses 2–19

O LORD, God of my deliverance, when I cry out in the night before You,
    let my prayer reach You; incline Your ear to my cry.
For I am sated with misfortune; I am at the brink of Sheol.
I am numbered with those who go down to the Pit;
    I am a helpless man abandoned among the dead,
    like bodies lying in the grave of whom You are mindful no more,
    and who are cut off from Your care.
You have put me at the bottom of the Pit,
    in the darkest places, in the depths.
Your fury lies heavy upon me; You afflict me with all Your breakers. *Selah.*
You make my companions shun me; You make me abhorrent to them;
    I am shut in and do not go out.
My eyes pine away from affliction; I call to You, O LORD, each day;
    I stretch out my hands to you.

Do You work wonders for the dead?
    Do the shades rise to praise You? *Selah.*
Is Your faithful care recounted in the grave,
    Your constancy in the place of perdition?
Are Your wonders made known in the netherworld,
    Your beneficent deeds in the land of oblivion?

As for me, I cry out to You, O LORD; each morning my prayer greets You.
Why, O LORD, do You reject me, do You hide Your face from me?
From my youth I have been afflicted and near death;
    I suffer Your terrors wherever I turn.
Your fury overwhelms me; Your terrors destroy me.
They swirl about me like water all day long; they encircle me on every side.
You have put friend and neighbor far from me and my companions out of my sight.

Psalm 103
Verses 1–5

Bless the LORD, O my soul, all my being, His holy name.
Bless the LORD, O my soul and do not forget all His bounties.
He forgives all your sins, heals all your diseases.
He redeems your life from the Pit, surrounds you with steadfast love and mercy.
He satisfies you with good things in the prime of life,
    so that your youth is renewed like the eagle's.

Psalm 116
Verses 1–9

I love the LORD for He hears my voice, my pleas;
    for He turns His ear to me whenever I call.
The bonds of death encompassed me; the torments of Sheol overtook me.
I came upon trouble and sorrow and I invoked the name of the LORD,
    "O LORD, save my life!"

The LORD is gracious and beneficent; our God is compassionate.
The LORD protects the simple; I was brought low and He saved me.
Be at rest, once again, O my soul, for the LORD has been good to you.
You have delivered me from death, my eyes from tears, my feet from stumbling.
I shall walk before the LORD in the lands of the living.

Psalm 121
A song for ascents

I turn my eyes to the mountains; from where will my help come?
My help comes from the LORD, maker of heaven and earth.
He will not let your foot give way; your guardian will not slumber;
See, the guardian of Israel neither slumbers nor sleeps!
The LORD is your guardian, the LORD is your protection at your right hand.
By day the sun will not strike you, nor the moon by night.
The LORD will guard you from all harm; He will guard your life.
The LORD will guard your going and coming now and forever.

Psalm 142
Verses 2–8

I cry aloud to the LORD; I appeal to the LORD loudly for mercy.
I pour out my complaint before Him; I lay my trouble before Him
    when my spirit fails within me.
You know my course; they have laid a trap in the path I walk.
Look at my right and see—I have no friend; there is nowhere I can flee,
    no one cares about me.
So I cry to You, O LORD; I say, "You are my refuge,
    all I have in the land of the living."
Listen to my cry, for I have been brought very low;
    save me from my pursuers, for they are too strong for me.
Free me from prison, that I may praise Your name.
The righteous shall glory in me for Your gracious dealings with me.

Modern Psalms

by Debbie Perlman

Debbie Perlman, the resident psalmist at Beth Emeth Free Synagogue in Evanston, Illinois, is the only full-time psalmist in America. Using the formulas and poetic sense of ancient psalms, Ms. Perlman writes modern psalms to reflect today's situations. Many of her psalms have a special focus on illness and healing.

The Torah reading *Parashat Bo* includes the description of the last three plagues visited upon the Egyptians. The penultimate plague, the plague of darkness, was said to have immobilized the Egyptians for three days. Sometimes a darkness we create in ourselves can have that same effect. We need then to open ourselves to God's light and illuminating force.

Two Hundred Forty-Six
The Plague of Darkness

> Deliver me from the darkness of my soul,
> Created by internal enemies, my defeaters;
> They shake the foundation of my being,
> They battle my innermost self.
>
> Not as day fades to evening, but as thieves they come,
> So abruptly they steal the light
> That I stand immobile, mute.
> Be again my Light, Holy One, as I seek the light.
>
> Strengthen the stars, remove the obscuring clouds,
> Unwrap the blindfold from my eyes;
> Renew in my spirit fortitude and strength,
> Your precious shard of brilliance, my sunrise.

Is it only serendipity that brings people to my website? One man wrote that he "did not know we still have psalmists in this day and age." And then: "What kind of psalm might be appropriate to heal a mentally and emotionally very disturbed, desperate, and unhappy woman?"—his ex-wife and the mother of his three-year-old daughter. "You don't need to respond to this e-mail," he went on, "but a psalm/prayer for Stella, daughter of Masha, just might be a good thing."

So I did what I do, sent him what he had so gently requested. He wrote back to thank me. I heard from him again today. He described the remarkable events of a pleasant afternoon with his ex-wife and daughter—"the very, very first time during Jenny's memorable life that she spent more than about one or two minutes of time together with both parents in the same room in happy conditions." A storm blew up, they returned to Stella's home, and Btzalel saw not one but two rainbows.

"What does it all mean?" He concluded, "I do not know. But your Psalm, our 'family' gathering with good feelings, the twin rainbow—all following so closely upon one another; all so very, very remarkable!"

Two Hundred Twenty-Three
A Song of Healing for Stella bat Masha

> Soothe these soul troubles, my Healer,
> Take my hand in courage;
> Embrace me with hope and calm,
> Lingering reminders of Your care.
> Let each new day bring progress,
> Aligning me toward wholeness.
>
> Bring strength and healing,
> A new day of brightness,
> Trouble-free nights of kind dreams.
>
> May I walk renewed in wonder
> At the person You have created,
> Senses attuned again to beauty,
> Hate and bitterness now set aside,
> A long journey safely ended.

I am amazed, again and again, by the power of cyberspace. A brief comment to my website can result in a burgeoning relationship as I reply and the e-mail begins. I adore that disembodied voice that announces that I've "got mail." I cherish the intimacies that flourish, the mutual support, the shared confidences.

Last year I made such a friend. A member of her synagogue's *Bikur Cholim* committee and an oncology social worker, she confided, as our correspondence continued, her anguish over her son's struggle with obsessive-compulsive disorder. Three months after our "meeting," a psalm appeared in my head. The image was so clear that I'm sure there was special guidance in its composition. She wrote me: "The story of Isaac, always moving and complicated, will have another deeper layer of meaning for me. I will draw strength and courage from your words since I believe that many of our connections to God come from our connections to other people."

We are electrons on a screen. We are part of a sacred community made possible by those bits and bytes.

One Hundred Seventy-Four
For Seth

Bound like Isaac upon the rock,
Held fast by thought terrors:
Mind grasping, pulse booming, gasping
Bands of breathlessness.

Where is the angel with the ram
Come to rescue this beloved son?
When will he arrive, loosening the bonds
That hold my child to the precipice?

I did not offer up my son,
Though my love for You is steadfast;
I cannot untie him,
Though my faith in You is firm.

Give us strengths, Almighty One,
To work free the mind-made knots,
Worrying them with our worries
Until a rush of wings clears the air.

Give us courages, Almighty One,
To cope with snarls and tangles;
Binds loosen and return,
Abide with us.

Eighty-Five
In Iyar: Ani Adonai Rofecha
A Song of Healing

After this long night of weakness,
I wake again in the morning of return;
Shaking off the terrors and the dreams,
I open my lips to the Eternal.

You are my Strength and my Hope,
The Author of my healing;
You are my Promise and my Courage,
Guiding the steps I take toward healing.

After the winter's darkness and biting cold,
The hidden awayness of my illness,
The isolation, the fear that settled upon me,
I rise with renewed strength to praise You.

You are the Wonder of new life,
Warming, healing sun upon my head;

You restore my concern for others,
As I relinquish my constant self-inventory.

You come to me as spring comes,
Circling back to heal the ravaged earth;
You rest Your hand of blessing on my shoulder
And I sigh with relief at Your concern.

I look for You, Divine Physician,
Even as I begin again to take up my life;
I look for You, Complete Healer,
As I begin again.

Making the decision to begin "talk therapy" is profound. It gets at the essence of who we are and asks that we start a process of revelation. Sometimes we will be filled with images that have been buried. Sometimes we will stumble in the memories. We begin the exploration, with God's help.

Two Hundred Fifty-One
Beginning Therapy

Today I will begin to uncover my heart,
I will let accumulations of sorrow surface;
Today the cycle of hurt and longing is suspended,
Arresting my spiral into the maelstrom.

If I falter, frightened of the struggle,
Be with me, my Staff and my Lamp;
Hold out a lantern of courage,
Fortify me, let me persevere.

All my yesterdays describe my future,
Yet I am more than their sum;
I begin the deciphering with trepidation,
Help me to calculate my strengths.

Mark this day with Your kindness,
Reassure my search for wholeness;
Give me patience as I take small steps,
Guide and vouchsafe my journey.

The young David was sent to play his music to soothe King Saul. What maladies had befallen the ruler? Since January I have been struggling with my own demons. Depression is a state that can paralyze. I find myself wondering what to do next, how to continue to put one foot before the other and move ahead. And I struggle to find words that will continue to sing my soul to God. What once came so easily, poured into me, has slowed to a trickle that requires all my concentration and effort. I know that this will eventually resolve, but for now, I am caught.

One Hundred Ninety-Nine
Depression

I awake bewildered.
As the last dream remnants fade,
And dawn expands to define the day,
I seek You.

Pull me up through clouds of ennui
That threaten my ability to sing to You.
Focus my heart to forge ahead;
Push away the stilled silence.

I am as a snared bird.
My wings cannot lift to flutter
Beyond the trap.
Free me from this weakness.

Fortify me with Your care,
For I am needy for strength;
Firm my loosened limbs
So my lips can open to honor You.

These Psalms, and many others, can be found online
at http://www.healingpsalm.com

Part 3

How May We Use Jewish Liturgy to Address Mental Illness in Our Communities?

Sample Sermons and Services

The sample sermons in this section, which were collected from all over the country, provide a variety of textual sources, timely contexts, and subject matters upon which to base a sermon on mental health. Following them are two services: "When Madness Comes Home: Prayer and Study in Anticipation of the End of the *Sheloshim*" and "*Havdalah* Healing Service," both of which address issues of mental health.

Introduction to a Sermon on Welcoming People Who Are Chronically Mentally Ill

Just a few weeks ago, we read these words from the Haggadah:

> Arami Oved Avi: My ancestor was a fugitive/wandering Aramean. He went down to Egypt and resided there in meager numbers and sojourned there; but there he became a great and very populous nation. The Egyptians dealt harshly with us and oppressed us; they imposed heavy labor upon us. We cried out to the Eternal, the God of our ancestors, and the Eternal heard our plea and saw our plight, our misery, and our oppression. The Eternal freed us from Egypt by a mighty hand, by an outstretched arm and awesome power, and by signs and by portents.

It's probably not so difficult for any of us to say, "My father, my grandfather, my grandmother was a fugitive, frightened, courageous, wandering Jew." You and I probably live in close enough proximity to have heard family stories of surviving day to day, barely tolerated at the margins of society, afraid to stick out lest viability bring down trouble, speaking a language that no one else understood.

Given that, it is only right that we look up from our *haggadot* to notice who the fugitive Arameans are today. I would posit that they are the chronically mentally ill. These fugitive Arameans live as many of our families did: at the edges, outside of normative society, anxiety provoking, and unwanted.

Truth to tell, there are many in our congregations who would just as soon not see *these* wandering Arameans wander too close, especially not into synagogue. But we're here to challenge the unspoken and embarrassing assumption that the synagogue is a place for all Jews except the "crazy ones."

Only part of our task is to welcome and help sustain people who are mentally ill. The other part is to build understanding and in that way create an atmosphere where every Jew is truly welcome.

Conquering Depression

by Rabbi Samuel M. Stahl

Depression affects all of us at one time or another. It can appear after the rejection of a friend or a lover, the loss of a job, the serious illness or death of a loved one, or numerous other traumas. Such depression is normal and begins to diminish as the crisis recedes.

However, there is another type of depression—one that is abnormal, devastating, and often lethal. It robs its victim of hope. It plunges one into a long-term, indescribable hell. It is not necessarily connected with a specific trauma. However, a trauma can ignite it in those who are predisposed to it.

This kind of depression has plagued people for centuries, even in the days of the Bible. Psalm 42 is a classic example. The Psalmist confesses that his tears have been his food day and night, because crying spells often accompany this kind of depression. Out of his anguish, the Psalmist poses this question to himself: "Why are you cast down, O my soul, and why do you moan within me?" This pathetic complaint clearly illustrates to what horrible psychic depths this biblical writer has sunk.

This kind of depression has afflicted some of the giants of the arts and of government. Among its victims have been Vincent van Gogh, Ernest Hemingway, Winston Churchill, and Abraham Lincoln. One of the most articulate sufferers of abnormal depression has been William Styron, author of the *Confessions of Nat Turner* and *Sophie's Choice*. Styron has also written *Darkness Visible: A Memoir of Madness,* which is a moving and gripping account of his morbid descent into the pits of depression.

Styron, in first person terms, vividly and graphically describes the torment suffered by the victim of abnormal depression. However, he acknowledges that even the greatest literary geniuses cannot fully convey in words the total intensity of its hell.

The causes of abnormal depression are mysterious. It can come from biochemical disturbances in the brain. It also has genetic roots. People affected by depression are grossly misunderstood. Loved ones grow impatient with them. They admonish them to "snap out of it," which is an impossible feat. Many depressives also feel a sense of shame or stigma. Such is unfortunate, because depression is an illness just like any other sickness.

But abnormal depression won't go away by itself. Styron himself was hospitalized for seven weeks, with a treatment plan that proved effective. There are three medical ways to combat depression: psychotherapy, medication, and electro-convulsive therapy, or shock treatments. But there is something that we, outside the medical community, can do to be helpful and supportive of depression.

One of the important adjuncts to medical treatment is for the victim to rediscover hope. In fact, the writer of Psalm 42 found enormous emotional release in crying out: "Hope in God. . . ." Hope is a central Jewish value. We Jews are called *asirei tikva,* "prisoners of hope." Therefore, close friends and family members of the victim need to encourage the sufferer to be hopeful. They should persuade him or her that life is basically worthwhile, that it is good to be alive.

—Samuel M. Stahl is Rabbi Emeritus of Temple Beth-El

San Antonio, Texas.

The Daily Struggle of Mental Illness

A Sermon at Bet Shalom, April 28, 2000

This past Sunday, I was at a funeral for one of the Holocaust survivors from the Friendship Club, a survivor group in Cincinnati, which I coordinate. The first time I met this woman was two months ago. It was not this group that brought us together, but rather a hospital visit. She was in the hospital for depression. We spent an hour or so talking and I learned about her life as a survivor and in coming to America. She revealed some of her likes and fears. She spoke of her family, her daughters and grandsons. The same night of our visit her husband died. She left the hospital for the funeral and did not return to the best of my knowledge. Last week she died of a stroke; it was not her depression that killed her, though it was a daily struggle to live with her diagnosis.

In the eulogy the rabbi mentioned her depression. In my mind I applauded his honesty, but then he blew it, because he mentioned a newspaper article he had read just that morning about a person with depression. I think he was trying to relate just how common clinical depression is. But then he continued. The article was about a woman who killed people in a car accident; the accident it seems was attributed to her depression, at least that is what I heard the rabbi communicate. Maybe the depression was the cause, maybe it was not. I did not see the article. Nevertheless, this type of example does not help the numbers of people living with and managing their depression, or whatever their diagnosis may be. Many who are at the top in their fields live secretly with this type of illness, for others may not understand it or may loose confidence in the performance ability of the person in question. This is not fair, but it does happen.

Not long ago, the following headline appeared across my computer screen: "Minnesota Governor Calls Suicide Action of 'Weak Minded.'" When I read this statement, which appeared in his *Playboy* magazine interview, one I admit I did not read in the original source, I knew it must be addressed for nothing could be further from the truth. His lack of sympathy for persons driven by brain disorders to commit suicide is an example of the ignorance and stigma that still needs to be overcome in American society regarding the treatment of mental illness.

If you learn nothing else this Shabbat, know that one who commits suicide is not at all "weak minded" but rather, more times than not, suffering from a mental illness that is either undiagnosed or diagnosed but, for whatever reason, not being treated effectively. Also, know that depression does not equal suicide. Depression does not mean violence. Depression does not mean complete withdrawal from society.

People with mental illness are not to be feared or treated differently from anyone else in this sanctuary. In fact, based on statistics, one in every four of us has a mental illness. So, it could be you, or you, or me.

Mental illness is not shameful though much of society may disagree. People are set in their ways and often form opinions based on stereotypes; change takes time. Don't forget, twenty-five years ago, cancer was spoken about in whispers. Today, awareness is high. I pray that this may also be the case with mental illness. Unfortunately, even during Mental Illness Awareness Week, the first week in October, the subject was not prevalent in the press; if it appeared it was a blip on the news or buried in the newspaper.

Thankfully not all people are as ignorant as Governor Ventura, who takes phobia and bias to an extreme. In the same interview I spoke about earlier, he admitted that he did not read books by Ernest Hemingway because the writer killed himself. Ernest Hemingway was known to be bipolar. By using suicide and the mental illness that sometimes precedes it as a method of measurement, Governor Ventura misses out on many great artists, composers, playwrights, authors, and musicians. In fact, in our own tradition it is thought that Reb Nachman of Bratzlav, a great mystical and inspirational rabbi, was bipolar. Who knows for sure, and who cares? This condition should not guide our choices.

Governor Ventura went on to say, "I've seen too many people fight for their lives. I have no respect for anyone who would kill himself. If you are a feeble, weak-minded person to begin with, I don't have time for you." When visiting Harvard University he was challenged on his remarks. He replied, "I don't have sympathy, is what my feelings are on suicide . . . to me it's something that doesn't have to happen if people take a positive attitude on life, like I do."

People who suffer with mental illness and contemplate or attempt suicide wish it was so easy "to take a positive attitude," but it is not. Mental illness is a no-fault brain disorder that destroys lives if left untreated or if the necessary support is not available. The rabbis of course did not realize the biological complexity of the brain, but they did have sympathy toward those who commit suicide. Though the halachah seems fixed on the concept that one who commits suicide is buried outside of the cemetery and not given a ritually complete funeral, most rabbis now will agree that these laws were set to discourage suicide and not to punish those who succeeded at committing suicide. In fact, when someone did kill himself the rabbis would often say he was not in the right frame of mind—*perhaps he was depressed*—and did not know what he was doing. And if he did not understand what he was doing, he did not consciously kill himself, and therefore his death was not suicide, but rather, an accident and he should be buried with honor.

The best example of this is found in a midrash about Saul. Saul committed suicide by falling on his own sword. The midrash begins, "And there was a famine in the days of David. . . . And the Lord said: 'It is because of Saul' (2 Samuel 21:1), because he was not mourned in the manner required by law." God continues to list all of the good that occurred during Saul's life and at once David gathers all the elders and notables of Israel together to go gather Saul's bones from across the Jordan, outside of the community. "They took the bones, put them in a coffin, and went back across the Jordan. Then David commanded that Saul's coffin be borne through the territory of each and every tribe. Upon the coffin's arrival in a tribe's territory, the entire tribe—the men, their sons, and daughters, as well as their wives—came out and paid affectionate tribute to Saul and his sons, thus discharging the obligation of loving-kindness to the dead. When the Holy One saw that Israel had shown such loving-kindness, He, immediately filled with compassion, sent down rain." In days of famine, this was truly a blessing.

God demonstrated compassion for a man who committed suicide. If we are all created in the image of God and we know that when faced with suicide God acted in a just and caring fashion, all the more so we should lend a helping and an empathetic ear to one who is in need, *before* suicide is even a thought.

Many will try to hide their illness, many will feel so ashamed that they do not seek help; this is what potentially leads to suicide, not weakness. The actress Margo Kidder tried to hide her illness with alcohol and drugs. When asked why, she explained that it is much more socially acceptable to admit to a substance problem than to mental illness. So many who admit to substance abuse use drugs and alcohol in an attempt to control their highs and lows without having to see a doctor, take their medication, or be labeled with the stigma of mental illness.

In addition, depression is the most common disorder and the leading cause of suicide among the elderly. "Men who are seventy-five years or older have the highest suicide rate of any age group, worldwide." I found this fact astounding. We often link suicide with teens but so many people in all age groups use it as an out when they are not able to penetrate their feelings of depression. None of us is immune.

It is not shameful to see a therapist or a psychiatrist. It is not shameful to take medication for a mental illness. One is not "weak-minded," in fact, just the opposite; it is quite courageous to get help and seek treatment. Seeing the signs in yourself or in someone you love and then asking for help or encouraging someone you love to seek help may be the most difficult hurdle.

In this community, Jewish Family and Children's Services of Minneapolis does have a Mental Health Support Services Department. Not every Jewish community is this far along. Also, clergy are available to make referrals. And though I have only one visit left after this weekend, I am happy to meet with anyone when I am at Bet Shalom. And I am happy to provide more information about mental illness. If I don't have the information with me, I will find it and share it with Rabbi Cohen to pass along.

This year I am in C.P.E. (Clinical Pastoral Education) and my supervisor mentioned that often the patients who don't get flowers or care packages of food are those with mental illness. He describes it as a "no-casserole disease," "the leprosy of our time." I am aware that often people do not admit mental illness, families may hide the diagnosis, and many people do not know what to do or say around someone with a mental illness. But realize your support helps. Direct questions help. The patient is often scared and alone and comments such as Governor Ventura's only complicate matters and fuel the fires of ignorance, thus adding to society's fears.

This ignorance must not be tolerated. I urge you, if someone you care about has a mental illness, to get help and offer your unequivocal support and encouragement. Silence is not the answer. Together we can break the stigma of mental illness and at the same time, I pray, lesson the rate of suicide.

At this season, slavery is a subject about which Jews are familiar. Our seders recall physical enslavement, but we realize that there is more than physical bondage. We are enslaved by different weights and measures. There are elements in our lives that tie us down and bind our ability to live life to the fullest. This Shabbat between Pesach and Yom HaShoah we can say as a Jewish community that we have known what it is like to be held captive and then set free. We also know that when we went out from Egypt, freedom was not easy. We moaned and complained and remembered Egypt in a different light.

So too with Holocaust survivors and liberation. Liberation simply marked a different struggle and a different battle to be won. Some survivors remember their pre-war days as perfect, and their deceased families as unflawed. But nothing is so black and white. These days our Jewish calendar teaches us that each stage of our journey offers different challenges and obstacles, but life does continue and many of us flourish.

Mental illness supports this pattern of slavery to freedom, bondage to liberation. Often one's life is controlled by the illness, bound if you will by such things as not knowing why moods change so quickly or why sadness or fear persists for no apparent reason. Upon diagnosis, many people feel a sense of exhilaration from knowing their behavior has a name. Others struggle because of societal pressure. Some question the diagnosis and acceptance comes slowly. Then the real work begins with the balancing of medications, coming to grips with the social stigma, and maybe even coping with loneliness, alienation, and the great fear of disclosure.

Next month begins Mental Health Awareness Month. Many people probably do not even realize there is such a month, but may be aware that October is Breast Cancer Awareness Month or, more likely, that March is a haven for basketball junkies. This is the reality of our society.

Let us not wait twenty-five years for the whispers of mental illness to blossom into our everyday conversation. Let us not shun therapy or therapists by calling them shrinks or quacks or any other derogatory terms.

I pray for the day when we all will feel free to speak openly about whatever ails our souls. I pray for the day when having a mental illness is not a stigma; when those with mental illness are applauded for their accomplishments and positive contributions to society. I pray that more public figures, like Tipper Gore, will stand up for those, including herself, who struggle with mental illness. I pray for the day when all the weight that such a diagnosis places on a person, his or her family, and friends becomes lighter with the proper caring and support.

May we at this season continue on our path from slavery to freedom by remembering those who are enslaved by society; those who know their diagnosis and wish they did not have to keep silent; those who think the world would be a better place if they were not part of it; those who are physically sick from medication while finding the right balance; those who are anything but weak-minded.

We can make a difference with openness, and acceptance, and understanding. If God was able to show compassion, may we also find the desire and strength to show compassion and break the stigma.

May it be God's will.

A No-Fault Disease

A Proposed Sermon

In general, physical illness is something we can see and identify. It is organic, and usually we can deal with physical illness without a great deal of guilt. Although we have made great strides in the area of mental illness, in the popular mind it is still often surrounded by myths, prejudices, and feelings of guilt. I am afraid that this may even be particularly true of Jews because we have traditionally prized the life of the mind and extolled intellectual achievement. Consequently, illnesses of the mind are still often seen in terms of embarrassment and failure, which are almost inevitably accompanied by shame and blame.

This attitude among Jews is a bitter irony because some of the greatest advancements in understanding mental and emotional illness have been made by Jews. At one time, the largest portion of psychoanalysts, psychiatrists, and therapists were Jews. Therefore, we should know better and should know more. I pray that this message tonight may make a small contribution toward furthering our understanding of mental illness.

In 1 Samuel 16, King Saul—our people's first monarch—is said to be tormented by "an evil spirit from God." Young David is introduced to the troubled king, who finds relief in David's presence and music. That which mystifies us, frightens us; the inexplicable even today, we sometimes explain as an evil spirit or divine punishment. Modern researchers have suggested that King Saul suffered from either manic depression or schizophrenia. More than music, David's willingness to befriend the king, his compassion and care even in the face of Saul's terrible rages, brought Saul peace and comfort.

Biblical prophets experienced trances and ecstasies. In antiquity, Jews interpreted such phenomena positively, as proof of divine contact. Our later tradition, however, treated reports of such experience negatively, as signs of illness, and Judaism sought to exorcise the ghosts or furies, *dybbuks,* that caused them. Music was often used in an attempt to seduce demons to leave the minds of the insane and thereby calm and cure them.

A diagnosis of insanity has legal implications in halachah—Jewish law. When the degree of mental incompetence warranted it, the Rabbis of the Talmud exempted the insane from responsibility in both religious and civil law. They made the insane ineligible for certain roles; for example, serving as another person's legal agent, or sometimes serving as a witness.

Listen to these early definitions from the Talmud. Who is deemed insane? He who goes out alone at night. He who spends the night in a cemetery. He who tears his garments. Rabbi Huna said he must do all of them to be considered insane. Rabbi Yochanan said he is to be considered insane even if does only one of them. Another definition of who is deemed insane is "one who destroys everything given to him." Maimonides, however, noted that these behaviors are to be constructed as symptoms, not as an exhaustive definition of insanity. Commentators continued to suggest specific criteria for determining mental disorders for purposes of legal excuse. Generally, loss of emotional control, or loss of the ability to reason or to make reality-based judgments became Judaism's operational definition of mental illness.

The general approach in Jewish sources was to disenfranchise the mentally ill, but not, however, to isolate them. Moreover, the rabbis distinguished between those times when a person was apparently sane and therefore legally capable, and those times in which he or she was not. But most important for our discussion, in Jewish legal literature mental illness is always classified as an illness rather than a moral fault. The Talmud permitted lighting a candle in violation of the Sabbath for a woman in labor in order to spare her psychic anguish. Citing that precedent, in the thirteenth century, Nachmanides specifically included mental illness in the category of *pikuach nefesh*—saving a life. Almost all obligations and prohibitions could be laid aside in order to save a person's mental as well as physical health. That view is seven hundred years old in Judaism.

The Jewish attitude became one of seeking prevention by offering advice for maintaining mental health. So, from the biblical Book of Proverbs to the rabbinic *Pirkei Avot* to the writings of Maimonides, Bachya ibn Pakuda, Luzzato, and others, there was an attempt to provide materials and lessons devoted to moral spiritual development. In such ways, Jews sought to prevent mental illness. However primitive our ancestors' understanding was, Jews saw mental illness not as something for which one should repent or be punished, but rather as a sickness we must seek to prevent or cure as part of our general obligation to heal. I believe it was this attitude that prepared the way for Sigmund Freud and many other Jews to develop and practice modern medical forms of psychological care.

We all know something about heart disease. We know about different types of cancer—breast cancer, prostate cancer, pancreatic cancer, lung cancer, colon cancer. We know about eye diseases, hearing loss, arthritis, which affects our mobility, osteoporosis, which affects our bones. The brain is also part of the body, and it too can become ill. Mental illness is a term used for a group of disorders causing severe disturbances in thinking, feeling, and relating. They result in substantially diminished capacity for coping with ordinary demands of life.

Mental illnesses range in severity from mild to disabling, can affect persons of all ages, and they can occur in any family. In America today, thirty-five million people suffer from some form of mental illness. One in four American families is affected by mental illness. In fact, more hospital beds in America are occupied by people who have mental illnesses than those who have cancer, heart trouble, and lung disease combined.

The causes of mental illness are not well understood, although it is believed today that the functioning of the brain's neurotransmitters is involved in a biochemical disorder. In other words, illness is due to a biochemical disturbance of the brain, not unlike the chemical changes that can cause a physical illness such as diabetes. Just as diabetes can be controlled but not cured with medication, so too can some of the symptoms of severe mental illness be controlled by proper medication.

Mental illness is not caused by dysfunctional families nor is it evidence of weakness of character. Heredity may be a factor in mental illness, as it is in diabetes and cancer. Stress may contribute to the onset of mental illness in vulnerable persons. Recreational drugs may also contribute to the onset, but they are unlikely to be the primary cause. While we surely do not have all the answers today, research to determine causes and to design strategies for prevention and rehabilitation is progressing, thank God. So, while there may not be cures for mental illness yet, proper treatment can substantially improve the functioning of many persons with mental illness and, in some cases, the patient may recover.

Mental illness is often temporary. A previously well-adjusted individual may have an episode of illness lasting weeks or months, and then may go for years or even a lifetime without another episode. Another may become ill periodically, yet between episodes be perfectly well.

Let me define four types of mental illnesses that we hear a great deal about, even as we don't necessarily understand their distinctions. The first is "affective disorders." This category is a big umbrella that covers the most common groupings of psychiatric disorders. The primary symptom is changed affect or mood. Mood disorders include manic depressive illness, what is often called "bipolar," in which the person swings between extreme high and low moods. Depression is also an affective disorder. Ten percent of Americans experience significant depression in their lifetime. At any given time, six in a hundred Americans—over fourteen million people—are diagnosed as having depression. Depression is most likely to strike people in the prime of life, ages twenty-five to forty-four, but can affect people of any age. Depression is diagnosed twice as often in women as in men. Severe depression is usually treated with a combination of cognitive therapy and medication, and with appropriate treatment, 80 percent of people with depression improve.

One of the most serious, complex, and disabling mental illnesses is schizophrenia. This disease affects men and women about equally. Its onset is usually in the late teens or twenties, rarely after age forty-five. About one in every one hundred Americans is affected by schizophrenia; each year one hundred thousand people are so diagnosed. Again, the cause of schizophrenia is a chemical imbalance in the brain or structural change within the brain. Research also cites a genetic predisposition as well as cultural, environmental, and psychological factors. Few generalizations hold true for everyone who has schizophrenia, but this much we do know today that we didn't know years ago—people with schizophrenia do not have a "split personality," and they are not prone to criminal violence. Their illness is not caused by bad parenting and is not evidence of weakness of character.

People experiencing an acute episode of schizophrenia have a sudden onset of severe psychotic symptoms. To be "psychotic" means to be out of touch with reality, or unable to separate real from unreal experience. Symptoms are eating and sleeping disorders, loss of motivation, hallucinations and delusions, poor concentration, and withdrawal. While medications can often control the most flamboyant symptoms of schizophrenia, none can cure it.

A third category of mental illness is anxiety disorders. We are not talking about the occasional tension, stress, and grief that accompany the emotional experiences of daily life. We are talking about a level of apprehension and tension that interferes with a person's ability to cope effectively with family, job, school, or other demands of daily life. As a group, anxiety disorders affect 8.3 percent of Americans. This group of illnesses includes phobias, panic disorders, post-traumatic stress disorder, and obsessive-compulsive disorders. Physical symptoms include excessive perspiration, shortness of breath, palpitations, rapid heartbeats, dizziness, tension headaches, and many other accelerated or slowed down bodily functions. There is no single situation or condition that causes anxiety disorders; rather, physical and environmental triggers often combine to create a particular anxiety illness. Medication, behavioral therapies, psychotherapy, or combinations thereof are used to treat these disorders and are highly effective.

Finally there is dementia. This group of diseases causes loss of intellectual abilities, especially memory, emotional shallowness, and personality changes. Alzheimer's disease, which affects 15 percent of people over age sixty-five, is included in this classification. Loss of nerve cells and brain atrophy are responsible for many of the dementias. A series of small strokes over a period of time can also result in the symptoms of dementia. Genetics seem to be a predisposing factor.

Dementia is not one of the things we worry about with young people, and this week's "Heads Up!" program has focused on young people, so let me return to youth and some troubling statistics. The second and third leading causes of death among teens between the ages of fifteen and nineteen are suicide and violence. In 1998 there were almost five hundred suicides in Oklahoma; a quarter of them involved young people under the age of twenty-five, and twenty of them were in Tulsa County. It is a myth that people who talk about killing themselves never really commit suicide; many do and many more give other warning signs. Suicidal people often feel life is hopeless; they talk about death and dying a lot and may give away prized possessions. It is important for us to know the warning signs.

This "Parents Guide to Mental Fitness," which will be available at the *Oneg,* starts out by saying: "Parenting is a tougher job today then it was for our parents." I believe that is true, and I urge you who are parents or grandparents to take a copy of this helpful guide home and read it. I want you also to know that this coming Wednesday night, for our high school students in Midrash and their parents, we shall have a special program in conjunction with "Heads Up!" We need to dispel the myth and stigma of mental or emotional illness. Let us remember that there is no shame in seeking professional help when we or members of our family are feeling depressed or otherwise emotionally ill. It is only a shame not to get help and to suffer needlessly.

A revolution has been taking place over the past thirty-five years or so in treatment of mental illness. Thirty-five years ago most of those needing care for serious mental illness were sent away to huge mental institutions. For hundreds of years before that they were quite literally "put away" in asylums, isolated from the community, often far from their homes and families. Since the 1960s, there has been a new trend in the treatment of mental illness. Those patients with severe mental illness who go to the better mental hospitals today receive intensive treatment; most are back with their families in a matter of a few months. Many continue to receive treatment while living at home. New drugs and new methods of treatment have made this possible.

In addition, mental health services are now being made more available in the community. These new services and methods of treatment are having far-reaching effects, not just on the mental patients, but on all of us. The distance that once separated us from the mentally ill is vanishing. It means that there are a growing number of mental patients or former patients in our community who are either completely restored or still in need of continued treatment while living and working within the community. Our attitude toward them, what we say and do when we are with them and their families, is all-important to their well-being.

Mental illnesses are just like other biological disorders; we should be able to discuss them just as openly as any other illness. Disclosure should not result in discrimination. Mental illness is a disability that responds to effective treatment. Lives may be saved by timely use of the best and most effective medicines and therapies. We must assure that these resources are available to all members of our community.

Therefore, let me make some concluding observations, which I hope will be of help. When mental illness strikes in any family it is unexpected and devastating—an experience not unlike a death in the family. The family must cope with and adapt to a terrible loss. Because of misunderstandings about mental illness, which still exist, it often can seem to be a humiliating event that brings shame to family members. Like all tragedies, mental illness raises the question "Why me?"; it may even initiate a challenge to a family's religious beliefs.

There is profound suffering with mental illnesses such as depression and schizophrenia. As I've said, the onset of these illnesses occurs frequently in late adolescence or early adulthood. It involves a major change in personality and social functioning and in coping with everyday problems. The victim is frequently affected by disturbing thoughts and feelings from which she or he cannot escape. For the family members, it often seems that the person they knew and loved, and for whom they had so many dreams, no longer exists. In that familiar person's place is a stranger whose behavior is unfathomable. The family lives in constant anxiety, often moving from crisis to crisis without respite.

When something terrible happens, it is normal to seek an appropriate source to blame. Many families go through stages of blaming the person for becoming ill and not getting better, or blaming the friends of the ill relative for being a bad influence or for abandoning the victim, or blaming the mental health professionals for not having a cure or giving helpful advice. Most of all, family members blame themselves for "causing" the problem or for not being able to "fix" it. It is not unusual for family members to go through intensive self-searching in an attempt to discover the "mistakes" or "sins" for which they feel they are being punished.

This preoccupation with responsibility sometimes even goes further. There is an obsessive concern "about doing the right thing" in the care and treatment of the person who has a mental illness. Families will agonize over every decision; they burden themselves with guilt each time things don't turn out as hoped.

And it is also a normal time to be angry with God. Like all senseless and unfair experiences, mental illness can shake one's belief in God. These are deeply unhappy moments. Many families who struggle with mental illness find this period a time of doubt, but they work through this period and come out with a more mature and meaningful relationship with God. Many Jewish families have moved from a faith that pleaded with God to remove the illness entirely to one that asks God for the serenity, the courage, and the wisdom to cope. It is human to hope for a miracle that will restore things to the way they were before the illness struck. Most families discover that the strength they have been given is the ability to withstand more emotional pain than they ever would have thought possible, to feel more in the midst of daily turmoil than was often felt in a more tranquil past, and a sense of being led to a wisdom greater than their own as they work their way through the maze of decisions that confront families who care for a person who has a mental illness. Acceptance is the key.

Mental illnesses are diseases of the brain; they are no-fault diseases. The challenge is not one of blame or shame, but of how to cope with and adapt to living with mental illness. As long as family members seek to escape their suffering through denial, through frantic searches for magical cures, or through blame, they condemn themselves and usually the loved one who has a mental illness to additional needless misery. Acceptance is not easy.

Acceptance means the ability to face the reality of illness, to learn about it, to learn about treatment, to have compassion for the person who has the mental illness, and to have compassion and forgiveness toward those who do not understand. Acceptance means the courage to no longer be ashamed of the illness, and a willingness to teach others that they might become more understanding and compassionate. Acceptance means "getting on" with one's own life and not allowing the illness to consume all the energies and resources of the family. It means attending to the needs of other family members who are not ill. It means trusting that one's own efforts are acceptable.

Often individuals begin by being so focused on their family problem that they have no time or energy for anything else. Acceptance begins when they start to turn outward, when they come to the realization that they can help establish God's dominion on Earth by working to improve the quality of life for those with mental illness. Some people, therefore, become active in organizations that support families of people with mental illnesses; others support research; others work to help identify and relieve people with mental illness; still others work in education and advocacy services.

I believe that our religious faith can bring healing even when curing is not possible. That healing involves serenity in the midst of tragedy; it involves courageous coping and compassionate caring. It is not a sudden miracle; it is something we work on achieving day by day in God's own time.

O, God, grant us the gift of acceptance that we might find courage to cope with the mental illness in our midst. Help us to learn the patience and understanding that people who have mental illness need. Help us not to victimize by uninformed and uncaring attitudes, but strengthen us to have the love and understanding to care for and nurture those people in need. Enable us to do Your will by reaching out to those who suffer, and let us say, Amen.

When Madness Comes Home

Prayer and Study
in Anticipation of the End of Sheloshim
Following the Death of J. Frank,
Sister of Miriam Frank[*]

Hine Ma Tov (sung in Hebrew)

הִנֵּה מַה-טּוֹב וּמַה-נָּעִים
שֶׁבֶת אַחִים גַּם-יָחַד

How good and sweet it is for brothers/sisters to sit together.[1]

Imagine what it's like to be a child whose profoundly depressed mother does not respond at all to a simple, "Look what I did in school today," or who suddenly switches moods, talking

---

[*]This service was prepared by Rabbi Margaret Moers Wenig and Dr. Miriam Frank, Beth Am, The People's Temple, New York, N.Y., June 1997.

Miriam's sister, J. Frank, had recently died of breast cancer while in her forties, but she had been mentally ill her entire adult life. Our hope was to make of J.'s memory a blessing by using this memorial service-of-sorts to help members of the congregation who were secretly struggling with mental illness in their own families. A year earlier our congregation had grieved following the suicide-death of the thirty-five-year-old son of a former president of Beth Am. Some of us knew the devastation his fifteen years of manic depression had wreaked on his family.

Rabbi Wenig knew many of the members of the congregation who had a mentally ill child, sibling, spouse, or parent, but most of those members did not know of each other's struggles. We hoped that this service would help bring the subject of mental illness out into the open, without putting anyone on the spot, or asking that anyone reveal painful family secrets in a public setting.

The printed version of this liturgy, which we actually used, included the Hebrew or Aramaic of the Prayers and Texts for Study. The passages from *When Madness Comes Home*, printed here in italics, were not *printed* in the liturgy but were simply read aloud at the points at which they appear in this version. (*When Madness Comes Home: Help and Hope for the Children, Siblings, and Partners of the Mentally Ill.* Copyright © 1977 by Victoria Secunda. Published by Hyperion. Permission granted to UAHC Press to reprint these excerpts from *When Madness Comes Home*. If you wish to reprint this material further contact the publisher's Subsidiary Rights Assistant, Jamie Terranova, at 212-633-4404.)

nonstop nonsense for thirty-six hours, and then disappears for months because she has to be hospitalized.

Imagine what it's like to be told by your father, before he goes to work each day, to keep an eye on your potentially suicidal mother when you get home from school—but he is so preoccupied that he never really explains what is going on, never asks how you are doing, and neither does anyone else . . .

Imagine that your psychopathic brother sexually molested you for years, but you never told your parents because they'd already been through so much with him—being lied to and bullied and unable to persuade him to see a psychiatrist and feeling like utter failures—that it would destroy them . . .

Imagine having an older sister, who is getting her doctorate in graduate school, steal your parents' credit cards during a visit home and spend thousands of dollars because, you later discover, she's in an uncontrollable manic state; the upshot is that your college tuition is gone and there's no way to get it back. But you mustn't hold it against her because she is, after all, "sick."

Now imagine that you are an adult, and you must tell the man or woman you've fallen in love with that you cannot move out of town because you must help look after your mentally ill parent since there's no decent, affordable place where he or she can be cared for. And, by the way, this thing may be genetic, so you're not sure you ought to have children . . .[2]

"My early memories of my family are really wonderful [says Liza]. I remember my mother brushing her hair before going out to a party and looking very beautiful. She and my father were madly in love. She had a luminous personality and great warmth—I adored her. Everyone did."

Liza's perfect life shattered when she was eleven. Within a period of six months, her mother toppled from gracious benevolence to howling madness—the most acute case of manic-depression her doctors had ever seen.

"I remember very vividly the last day she lived at home. She went berserk at the breakfast table with my father. He was trying to calm her down, and suddenly they were locked in a terrible physical battle. I knew this was just horrible. Horrible. Horrible. My little brother was hustled out of the room by a maid. But I had to go to school. So I went out into the hall to get the elevator, and stood streaming with tears, because there was nobody who could comfort me."[3]

All of the individuals who read aloud portions of this liturgy (including the excerpts from Allen Ginsberg's "Kaddish") were family members of someone with mental illness, or struggled with mental illness themselves (although they were not publicly identified as such).

After the service many people revealed, in one-on-one conversations, that they too had a "crazy" family member. Others just said, "Thank you. That was a great service."

A few years after this service I received the following e-mail message from a Beth Am member who had been there: "I attended the service at a time when I was struggling to keep from fracturing a relationship with a very close relative whose mental health was at the core of the problem between us. I remember very little in specific about the liturgy, but I remember clearly feeling a physical relief from the anger I felt at this person. I remember finally understanding, after years of distress and conflict, that the fault lay neither with this person nor with me. That understanding transformed this relationship for me. Although the same issues still exist, things have never gotten so bad again."

[1]"How good and sweet it is for brothers/sisters to sit together." The members of Beth Am begin and end every shivah minyan, in our community, singing this verse.

[2]*When Madness Comes Home* (hereafter, *WMCH*), pp. 4–5.

[3]*WMCH*, pp. 49–50.

"My soul was just destroyed by my daughter's illness. It was more than just rupturing. It killed me. For many years I blamed myself and withdrew from everyone, because I couldn't bear the pain. I even fired God."[4]

Psalm 88[5]

O God of my deliverance,
when I cry out in the night before You
let my prayer reach You;
incline Your ear to my cry,
For I am sated with misfortune;
I am at the brink of Sheol.
I am numbered with those who go down to the Pit;
I am like one who has lost all strength
wandering freely among the dead,
like bodies lying in the grave
whom You remember no more,
who are cut off from Your loving hand.
You have laid me low,
at the bottom of the Pit,
in the dark, in the depths.

[Why] does Your fury fall heavy upon me?
[Why] do You afflict me in wave after wave?
[Why] do You make my companions shun me?
[Why] do You make me abhorrent to them?

I am shut in and cannot go out.
My eyes pine away from affliction.
I call to You, O God, each day;
I stretch out my hands to You.

Will You do wonders for the dead?
Will the shadows rise and praise You?
Shall Your steadfast love be reported in the grave,
Your faithfulness among the lost souls?

Are Your wonders made known in the darkness?
Your righteousness in the land of the forgotten?

---

[4]*WMCH,* p. 123
[5]Ps. 88 expresses the desperation, anger, and loneliness of some who are mentally ill and also of their parents, children, siblings, and partners who often do not tell their friends about the terror in their lives.

And I, to You have I cried O God;
In the morning my prayer greets You.

Why, O God have You abandoned my soul?
Why do You hide Your face from me?

From my youth I have been afflicted and near death.
I suffer Your terrors, I am numb.
Your wrath overwhelms me;
Your terrors destroy me.
They swirl around me all day long;
they surround me on all sides.
You have distanced lover and neighbor from me.
Those who know me are in darkness.

Texts for Study

Blessing on Torah Study (recited in Hebrew)

בָּרוּךְ אַתָּה, יְיָ אֱלֹהֵינוּ, מֶלֶךְ הָעוֹלָם, אֲשֶׁר קִדְּשָׁנוּ בְּמִצְוֹתָיו
וְצִוָּנוּ לַעֲסוֹק בְּדִבְרֵי תוֹרָה.

Mishnah Haggigah 1:1[6] (Hebrew text is read and studied)

(א) הכל חייבין בראיה, חוץ מחרש, שוטה וקטן, וטומטום, ואנדרוגינוס,
ונשים, ועבדים שאינם משוחררים, החגר, והסומא, והחולה, והזקן, ומי
שאינו יכול לעלות ברגליו. איזהו קטן, כל שאינו יכול לרכוב על כתפיו
של אביו ולעלות מירושלים להר הבית, דברי בית שמאי. ובית הלל
אומרים, כל שאינו יכול לאחוז בידו של אביו ולעלות מירושלים להר
הבית, שנאמר, שלש רגלים:

All are required to appear before the Lord (Exod. 23:14; Deut. 16:16) except for a *cheresh* (deaf-mute),[7] a *shoteh*,[8] a minor, one without pronounced sexual characteristics, one who

---

[6]This mishnah acknowledges that there are those who cannot, in all fairness, be held liable for fulfilling certain adult responsibilities, for all sorts of reasons: physical disability, competing responsibilities, and mental/psychological disability.

[7]The status of the deaf-mute, in Jewish law, changed dramatically in the 1800s when a legal authority visited a school for the deaf and discovered that a deaf-mute might indeed be *compos mentis*.

[8]Some translate *shoteh* as "imbecile" or "idiot," others as "insane." According to Marcus Jastrow's *Dictionary of the Targum, Talmud Babli, Yerushalmi, and Midrashic Literature*, *shoteh* is a "madman," a "fool," from the verb *sh-t-h*, to go astray, to be or to become demented, to be mad, to rage, to be impassioned; a *bar shoteh* is one "subject to attacks of insanity." The *Even Shoshan* Hebrew/Hebrew dictionary defines *shoteh* as both an idiot *and* as one who is not *shafui b'daato*, lit. sane/balanced in his mind or idiomatically, "in his right mind."

exhibits the sexual traits of both sexes, women,[9] slaves who have not been freed, the lame, the blind, the sick, the old, and one who cannot go up on foot.

Tosefta, Terumot 1:3 (Hebrew text is read and studied)

‫3. איזה הוא‬

‫שוטה, היוצא יחידי בלילה, והלן בבית הקברות, והמקרע את כסותו, והמאבד‬
‫מה שנותנין לו. פעמים שוטה, פעמים חלום, זה הכלל כל זמן ששוטה הרי הוא‬
‫כשוטה לכל דבר, וחלום, הרי הוא בפיקח לכל דבר.‬

Who is a *shoteh?*
One who goes out alone at night, and walks about in the cemetery,
and one who tears his clothes, and one who destroys what has been given to him.[10]

Babylonian Talmud, Haggigah 3b, 4a[11] (Hebrew/Aramaic text is read and studied)

‫איזהו שוטה? היוצא יחידי בלילה, והלן בבית הקברות, והמקרע את‬
‫כסותו. איתמר, רב הונא אמר: עד שיהו כולן בבת אחת. רבי יוחנן‬
‫אמר: אפילו באחת מהן. היכי דמי? אי דעביד להו דרך שטות - אפילו‬
‫בחדא נמי. אי דלא עביד להו דרך שטות - אפילו כולהו נמי לא! -‬
‫לעולם דקא עביד להו דרך שטות, והלן בבית הקברות - אימור כדי‬
‫שתשרה עליו רוח טומאה הוא דקא עביד, והיוצא יחידי בלילה - אימור‬
‫גנדריפס אחדיה, והמקרע את כסותו - אימור בעל מחשבות הוא. כיון‬
‫דעבדינהו לכולהו - הוה להו‬

‫כמי שנגח שור חמור וגמל, ונעשה מועד לכל. אמר רב פפא: אי שמיע‬
‫ליה לרב הונא הא דתניא: אי זהו שוטה - זה המאבד כל מה שנותנים‬
‫לו, הוה הדר ביה. איבעיא להו:‬

Who is deemed an imbecile [a *shoteh*]?
One who goes out alone at night and one who spends the night in a cemetery and one who tears his garments.
It was taught: R. Huna said: They must all be done together.

---

[9]You might find it curious that feminists would quote Jewish legal sources on the mentally ill, which are some of the very sources used to disenfranchise women. We study these sources here not because we consider them absolutely authoritative or prescriptive, but because they are evidence that the tradition knew of and spoke about the mentally ill. To Jews who have been keeping secret the mental illness in their families, it is liberating to learn that our tradition was not silent on the subject.
[10]This *Tosefta* understands *shoteh* to be not simply one who is mentally retarded but one who acts wildly.
[11]The Gemara quotes the *Tosefta*'s understanding of the *shoteh,* but notices an ambiguity: How wild/crazy does a person have to act to be considered a *shoteh?* The Gemara's discussion of this question is, in effect, an attempt to develop diagnostic criteria.

R. Yochanan said: Even if he does only one of them.

What is the case?

If he does them in an insane manner, even one [of these actions] is also [proof].

If he does none of them in an insane manner, even doing all of them proves nothing. . . .

R. Papa said: If R. Huna had heard of that which is taught [in the Tosefta]: Who is deemed an imbecile? . . . "One who destroys all that is given to him," he would have retracted.

From the *Mishneh Torah* of Maimonides[12]:

Sacrifices, Pilgrim Offering 2:1 (Hebrew text is read and studied)

א **נשים** יועבדים פטורין מן הראייה . וכל האנשים חייבים בראייה חוץ מחרש וא
ושוטה וקטן וסומא ותגר וטמא וערל . וכן הזקן והחולה והרך והענוג מאד שא'
יכולים לעלות על רגליהן כל אלו האחד עשר פטורין .

Women and slaves are exempt from appearance in the Temple. But it is required of all men to appear in the Temple as pilgrims, unless one is deaf, speechless, *shoteh* insane, or a minor, or blind, lame, unclean, or uncircumcised. So too, the aged and the sick, the very tender and delicate, who cannot go up to the Temple on their own feet. All these eleven are exempt.

Acquisition, Sales 29:4, 5 (Hebrew text is read and studied)

ד **י**חשוטה אין מקחו
מקח ואין ממכרו ממכר . ואין מתנותיו קיימות . ובית
דין מעמידים אפטרופום לשומים כדרך שמעמידין
לקטנים: **ה** מי שהוא עת שוטה ועת שפוי כגון אלו הנכפין . בעת שהוא שפוי כל
מעשיו קיימין חוכת לעצמו ולאחרים ככל בן דעת . וצריכין העדים לחקור הדבר היטב
שמא בסוף שטותו או בתחלת שטותו עשה מה שעשה:

Neither the purchase nor the sale of [i.e., by] an imbecile [a *shoteh*] is valid, nor are his gifts valid. The court appoints an administrator for imbeciles as it does for minors.[13]

For one who is alternately insane and sane, as in the case of epileptics, the rule is that when he is sane all his dealings are valid and he may acquire ownership for himself and for others like any sensible person. The witnesses should investigate the matter thoroughly to be sure that he did not perform the act toward the end or at the beginning of his lapse into insanity.

---

[12]*Mishneh Torah: Maimonides' Code of Law and Ethics,* abridged and translated from the Hebrew by Philip Birnbaum, Hebrew Publishing Company, New York, 1944, 1967, 1974. Note the varied/inconsistent translation of *shoteh,* sometimes: "imbecile," sometimes "insane."

[13]Not only is a *shoteh* exempt from certain ritual obligations incumbent upon an adult male, the *shoteh* is also not considered a responsible adult in matters of civil law.

Knowledge, Repentance, 5:1 (Hebrew text is read and studied)

א רְשׁוּת לכל אדם נתונה אם רצה להטות עצמו לדרך טובה ולהיות צדיק הרשות בידו . ואם רצה להטות עצמו
לדרך רעה ולהיות רשע הרשות בידו . הוא שכתוב בתורה הן האדם היה כאחד ממנו לדעת טוב ורע . כלומר
הן מין זה של אדם היה יחיד בעולם ואין מין שני דומה לו בזה העניין שיהא הוא מעצמו בדעתו ובמחשבתו יודע הטוב
והרע ועושה כל מה שהוא חפץ ואין מי שיעכב בידו מלעשות הטוב או הרע וכיון שכן הוא פן ישלח ידו :

Free will is granted to every human being. If a man wants to follow the good path and be
good, he has the power to do so; if he wants to follow the evil way and be wicked, he is
free to do so. It is written, "Indeed, man has become like one of us, knowing good and evil."
That is to say, the human species is unique in the world, there being no other species like
it in this respect, namely that man by himself, using his own intelligence and reason, knows
what is good and what is evil, without anyone preventing him from doing good or evil as
he pleases . . .

*"I guess I just snapped, because nothing I did made any difference. I said to [my schizophrenic
brother], 'That's it. You're on your own. You can figure out how to get your Social Security pay-
ments, where to live, how to make bail. I am finished with you.' Well, within twenty-four hours
he got himself into treatment. He's living in a halfway house where he follows the rules. He's no
longer violent. He's clean and takes his meds. Mentally ill people are capable of some volition,
some rational thinking. I can't tell you how much better I feel about him. I really look forward
to seeing him now, because he's helping himself."*[14]

*Imagine what it's like to have your mother, who has schizophrenia but won't take her pills, sud-
denly come thundering into your room to scream at you for sassing her, when in reality it's the
voices in her head that are taunting her.*[15]

Damages, Assault, and Battery 4:20[16] (Hebrew text is read and studied)

ב "חרש שוטה וקטן פגיעתן רעה
החובל בהן חייב והן שחבלו
באחרים פטורין . אע״פ שנתפתח החרש ונשתפה השוטה
והגדיל הקטן אינם חייבין לשלם שבשעה שחבלו בהן
לא היו בני דעת :

---

[14]*WMCH,* p. 269.
[15]*WMCH,* p. 4
[16]Maimonides, who believed in human free will, struggled to find the appropriate balance between holding a *shoteh*
responsible for his actions and excusing him from responsibility for his actions.

It is harmful *[sic]*[17] to clash with a deaf-mute, an imbecile *[shoteh]*, or a minor; if a man injures one of these he is held liable; if they injure other people, they are exempt. Even after a deaf-mute has been cured of his defect, or an imbecile has become normal, or a minor has grown up, he is not held liable for payment, because none of these was sensible when he inflicted the injury.

Damages, Assault, and Battery 5:1 (Hebrew text is read and studied)

א אסור לאדם לחבל בין בעצמו בין בחבירו .

A man is forbidden to injure himself or another.[18]

Prayers

"It's a trust issue. It's hard to trust anybody when the people you were closest to as a kid could just go away. What that teaches you is that the world is not a safe place. So you become emotionally removed. Yet I never thought I'd reach the age of forty-seven and still be unmarried. I'd really like to have a woman in my life. But somehow, I don't do anything about it. I can't figure it out."[19]

Mi Shebeirach

May God who blessed our fathers and mothers,
Abraham, Isaac and Jacob, Sarah, Rebecca, Rachel and Leah,
grant blessed healing to all those members of our congregation
and members of our families
who struggle with mental illness.
May God be with them in their illness
and give them patience, hope, and courage.
May God so endow their attending physicians and therapists with insight and skill
that they be soon restored to health and vigor of body and mind.
May God be with their families too
and grant them patience, hope, and courage.
May God remove their anger and wipe away their feelings of guilt.
May God endow them with a full life and with love
that they too enjoy health and vigor of body and mind.

---

[17]Translate instead: Whoever seriously *(raah)* hurts a *cheresh*, a *shoteh*, or a *katan* . . . or: Hurting a *cheresh*, a *shoteh*, or a *katan* is evil *(raah)*.

[18]Given that "a man is forbidden to injure himself *or another*," why was it necessary for the tradition to teach us that it is forbidden to injure a *cheresh*, a *shoteh*, or a *katan?* Wouldn't the latter be included in the former? Perhaps it is necessary to remind us that it is forbidden to hurt a *shoteh*, for example, because caring for a *shoteh* can make one angry or frustrated enough to want to hurt him. Or perhaps it is necessary to remind us that even though the *shoteh* does not behave as a "normal human being" none the less he is entitled to be treated as a human being and not as somehow less than human.

[19]*WMCH*, p. 219.

May God bind up their wounds
that they may enjoy many a *simchah* and thank God
for the blessings of health, let us say, Amen.[20]

"My brother's sleep cycles were completely off. He'd walk around the house in the middle of the night screaming and pounding on walls and doing crazy, raving things. When my dad was out of town, I'd stand watch while my mom slept, then grab a couple of hours of sleep when she woke up. From the age of fourteen until I went to college, I lived in fear not so much for myself, but for my mother. I even took a martial arts course so I could protect her."[21]

Night Time Prayer: (Hashkiveinu is sung in Hebrew)

הַשְׁכִּיבֵנוּ, יְיָ אֱלֹהֵינוּ, לְשָׁלוֹם וְהַעֲמִידֵנוּ, מַלְכֵּנוּ, לְחַיִּים.
וּפְרוֹשׂ עָלֵינוּ סֻכַּת שְׁלוֹמֶךָ, וְתַקְּנֵנוּ בְּעֵצָה טוֹבָה מִלְּפָנֶיךָ,
וְהוֹשִׁיעֵנוּ לְמַעַן שְׁמֶךָ, וְהָגֵן בַּעֲדֵנוּ. וְהָסֵר מֵעָלֵינוּ אוֹיֵב,
דֶּבֶר וְחֶרֶב וְרָעָב וְיָגוֹן; וְהָסֵר שָׂטָן מִלְּפָנֵינוּ וּמֵאַחֲרֵינוּ;
וּבְצֵל כְּנָפֶיךָ תַּסְתִּירֵנוּ, כִּי אֵל שׁוֹמְרֵנוּ וּמַצִּילֵנוּ אָתָּה, כִּי
אֵל מֶלֶךְ חַנּוּן וְרַחוּם אָתָּה. וּשְׁמוֹר צֵאתֵנוּ וּבוֹאֵנוּ לְחַיִּים
וּלְשָׁלוֹם, מֵעַתָּה וְעַד עוֹלָם. בָּרוּךְ אַתָּה, יְיָ, שׁוֹמֵר עַמּוֹ
יִשְׂרָאֵל לָעַד.

Grant, Eternal our God, that we lie down in peace
and rise again, O Sovereign God, to life.
Spread over us Your shelter of peace,
and guide us with Your good counsel.
Save us, for Your name's sake; shield us. Shield us.
Remove from us every enemy, plague, sword, famine, and grief.
Keep Satan from leading or pursuing us.[22]
In the shadow of Your wings shelter us.

For a protecting and saving God are You.
For a loving and merciful God are you.

---

[20]Adapted from *Sabbath Prayer Book,* The Jewish Reconstructionist Foundation, Inc., New York, 1965, p. 491
[21]*WMCH,* pp. 145–46
[22]Satan is here understood to be the psychological demons or phantoms that can plague us: anxiety, depression, mania, paranoia, psychoses . . . or even a dangerous family member who is plagued by one of those demons.

Guard our going and our coming
that we have life and peace, now and always.
Spread over us Your shelter of peace.

"It's been six years since my mother killed herself, and I still have nightmares about it."[23]

Night Time Prayer[24]: (recited in Hebrew)

בָּרוּךְ אַתָּה יהוה אֱלֹהֵינוּ מֶלֶךְ הָעוֹלָם, הַמַּפִּיל
חֶבְלֵי שֵׁנָה עַל עֵינַי וּתְנוּמָה עַל עַפְעַפָּי. וִיהִי
רָצוֹן מִלְּפָנֶיךָ יהוה אֱלֹהַי וֵאלֹהֵי אֲבוֹתַי,
שֶׁתַּשְׁכִּיבֵנִי לְשָׁלוֹם וְתַעֲמִידֵנִי לְשָׁלוֹם, וְאַל
יְבַהֲלוּנִי רַעְיוֹנַי וַחֲלוֹמוֹת רָעִים וְהִרְהוּרִים רָעִים,
וּתְהִי מִטָּתִי שְׁלֵמָה לְפָנֶיךָ, וְהָאֵר עֵינַי פֶּן אִישַׁן
הַמָּוֶת, כִּי אַתָּה הַמֵּאִיר לְאִישׁוֹן בַּת עָיִן. בָּרוּךְ
אַתָּה יהוה, הַמֵּאִיר לָעוֹלָם כֻּלּוֹ בִּכְבוֹדוֹ.

May it be Your will, Eternal my God
and God of my mothers and fathers,
that I lie down in peace and rise again in peace.
Let no disturbing thoughts come to upset me,
nor evil dreams, or evil thoughts.
May I know a peaceful rest.
And in the morning may You awaken me to the light of a new day.

Norma . . . whose mother had severe manic-depression, was the custodian in her family. . . .
Her father, who couldn't cope with her mother's mental illness, would rush out the door each
morning, leaving behind a "to-do" list for Norma. The strain of having to care for her mother,
her siblings, and the household was so great that by the time she was nineteen, she had an ulcer
and was spitting up blood.

---

[23]*WMCH*, p. 254
[24]Adapted from "Kriyat Sh'ma Al Ha Mita" (Prayer on retiring for the night), *HaSiddur*, translated and arranged by
Ben Zion Bokser, Behrman House, New York, 1983, p. 375.

One day, while driving on a highway, it occurred to her that by flooring the accelerator and veering off a bridge, her troubles would be over. But then she recalls: "This voice in my head said, 'Go to Elaine,' my best friend. I went over to her house and told her the whole story. . . . She said, 'You've got two choices: You can either tell your father to get on the stick and deal with your mother, or you can leave.' I said, 'I can't leave.' She said, 'Yes, you can. We'll do it together.' She literally dragged me out of the house and helped me find an apartment. When I moved out, I was finally able to sleep at night. I could concentrate on making myself well. I had a best friend to watch over me—she was my guardian angel. From then on, I got stronger, and my health came back."[25]

Night Time Prayer[26]: (sung in Hebrew)

בְּשֵׁם יהוה אֱלֹהֵי יִשְׂרָאֵל, מִימִינִי מִיכָאֵל, וּמִשְּׂמֹאלִי גַּבְרִיאֵל, וּמִלְּפָנַי אוּרִיאֵל, וּמֵאֲחוֹרַי רְפָאֵל, וְעַל רֹאשִׁי שְׁכִינַת אֵל.

In the name of God, may Michael be at my right hand, and Gabriel at my left; before me Uriel; behind me Raphael; and above my head God's presence.

"My greatest fear was that what happened to my mother would happen to me, and by God, nobody was going to put me in a psych hospital. I didn't have any friends because I was afraid that if people got to know me, they'd see the flaws in my character and lock me away. I buried all my emotions. My saving grace was walking in the hills near the farm where I grew up. The one place I could allow myself to have emotions was a big rock in the woods. I would go to that rock and try to get in touch with the anger and the pain. It reached a point that I invented a woman who, in my mind, would walk up the trail and sit beside me on the rock and talk to me. She'd put her arm around me and say, 'I care about what's happening to you.' I went to that rock every chance I got."[27]

[25]*WMCH,* pp. 147–48

[26]From "Night Prayer," *Hasiddur Hashalem,* translated and annotated by Philip Birnbaum, Hebrew Publishing Company, New York, 1949, 1977, p. 784

[27]*WMCH,* p. 144

Psalm 121[28] (sung in Hebrew)

שִׁיר לַמַּעֲלוֹת

אֶשָּׂא עֵינַי אֶל־הֶהָרִים
מֵאַיִן יָבֹא עֶזְרִי:
2 עֶזְרִי מֵעִם יְהוָה
עֹשֵׂה שָׁמַיִם וָאָרֶץ:
3 אַל־יִתֵּן לַמּוֹט רַגְלֶךָ
אַל־יָנוּם שֹׁמְרֶךָ:
4 הִנֵּה לֹא־יָנוּם וְלֹא יִישָׁן
שׁוֹמֵר יִשְׂרָאֵל:
5 יְהוָה שֹׁמְרֶךָ
יְהוָה צִלְּךָ
עַל־יַד יְמִינֶךָ:
6 יוֹמָם הַשֶּׁמֶשׁ לֹא־יַכֶּכָּה
וְיָרֵחַ בַּלָּיְלָה:
7 יְהוָה יִשְׁמָרְךָ מִכָּל־רָע
יִשְׁמֹר אֶת־נַפְשֶׁךָ:
8 יְהוָה יִשְׁמָר־צֵאתְךָ וּבוֹאֶךָ
מֵעַתָּה וְעַד־עוֹלָם:

I will lift up my eyes to the hills
from whence shall my help come.

My help comes from God,
Creator of heaven and earth.

God will not suffer your foot to be moved.
The one who watches over you will not slumber.

Behold, the one who watches over Israel
will neither slumber nor sleep.

---

[28]Miriam found great comfort in reciting this psalm. It offers hope that it is indeed possible to survive even the most trying of times.

God watches over you.
God is the shade by your right hand.

The sun shall not smite you by day
nor the moon by night.

God will protect you through all evil.
God will protect your soul.

God will watch over your going out and your coming in
from this time forth, and for evermore.

In Memory of J. Frank

Miriam Speaks about Her Sister

Zichrona livracha. May her memory be a blessing.

Kaddish
    From "Kaddish for Naomi Ginsberg 1894–1956"
    by Allen Ginsberg[29]

    Strange now to think of you, gone . . .

    I've been up
        all night, talking, talking, reading the *Kaddish* aloud,
        listening to Ray Charles blues shout blind on the phonograph . . .

    Dreaming back thru life, Your time—and mine accelerating
        toward Apocalypse . . .

    looking back . . .

    sighing, screaming with it, buying and selling pieces of phantom,
        worshipping each other, . . .

    education marriage nervous breakdown, operation,
        teaching school, and learning to be mad, in a dream—
        what is this life? . . .

---

[29] *Kaddish and Other Poems 1958–1960,* by Allen Ginsberg, City Lights Books, 1961, is a vivid testimony from the son of a woman who was mentally ill. Permission for one-time use only granted to UAHC Press by HarperCollins Publishers, Inc. For permission to use on some other occasion, contact: Permissions Department, HarperCollins Publishers, Inc., 10 East 53rd St., 12th Floor, New York, NY, 10022-5299.

What came is gone forever every time—
That's good! That leaves it open for no regret—no fear
radiators, lacklove, torture even toothache in the end—
Though while it comes it is a lion that eats the soul—and the
lamb, the soul, in us, alas, offering itself in sacrifice to
change's fierce hunger—hair and teeth—and the roar
of bonepain, skull bear, break rib, rot-skin, braintricked
Implacability.

Ai! ai! we do worse! We are in a fix! And you're out, Death
let you out, Death had the Mercy, you're done with your
century, done with God, done with the path thru it—
Done with yourself at last—Pure—Back to the Babe
dark before your Father, before us all—before the
world—

There, rest. No more suffering for you. I know where you've
gone, it's good.

All the accumulations of life, that wear us out—clocks, bodies,
consciousness, shoe, breasts—begotten sons—your Communism—
"Paranoia" into hospitals. . . .

This is the end, the redemption from Wilderness, way for
the Wonderer, House sought for All, black handkerchief washed
clean by weeping—page beyond Psalm—Last change of mine
and Naomi—to God's perfect Darkness—Death, stay thy phantoms!

El Moley Rachamim (sung in Hebrew)

Recited in memory of a man.

אֵל מָלֵא רַחֲמִים. שׁוֹכֵן בַּמְּרוֹמִים. הַמְצֵא מְנוּחָה נְכוֹנָה תַּחַת כַּנְפֵי
הַשְּׁכִינָה. בְּמַעֲלוֹת קְדוֹשִׁים וּטְהוֹרִים. כְּזֹהַר הָרָקִיעַ מַזְהִירִים. אֶת־נִשְׁמַת . . .
שֶׁהָלַךְ לְעוֹלָמוֹ: בַּעֲבוּר שֶׁאֲנִי *נוֹדֵר צְדָקָה בְּעַד הַזְכָּרַת נִשְׁמָתוֹ. בְּגַן עֵדֶן
תְּהֵא מְנוּחָתוֹ: לָכֵן בַּעַל הָרַחֲמִים יַסְתִּירֵהוּ בְּסֵתֶר כְּנָפָיו לְעוֹלָמִים. וְיִצְרוֹר
בִּצְרוֹר הַחַיִּים אֶת־נִשְׁמָתוֹ. יְיָ הוּא נַחֲלָתוֹ. וְיָנוּחַ עַל־מִשְׁכָּבוֹ בְּשָׁלוֹם. וְנֹאמַר

Recited in memory of a woman.

אֵל מָלֵא רַחֲמִים. שׁוֹכֵן בַּמְּרוֹמִים. הַמְצֵא מְנוּחָה נְכוֹנָה תַּחַת כַּנְפֵי
הַשְּׁכִינָה. בְּמַעֲלוֹת קְדוֹשִׁים וּטְהוֹרִים. כְּזֹהַר הָרָקִיעַ מַזְהִירִים. אֶת־נִשְׁמַת . . .
שֶׁהָלְכָה לְעוֹלָמָהּ: בַּעֲבוּר שֶׁאֲנִי *נוֹדֵר צְדָקָה בְּעַד הַזְכָּרַת נִשְׁמָתָהּ. בְּגַן עֵדֶן

תְּהֵא מְנוּחָתָהּ: לָכֵן בַּעַל הָרַחֲמִים יַסְתִּירֶהָ בְּסֵתֶר כְּנָפָיו לְעוֹלָמִים. וְיִצְרוֹר בִּצְרוֹר הַחַיִּים אֶת־נִשְׁמָתָהּ. יְיָ הוּא נַחֲלָתָהּ. וְתָנוּחַ עַל־מִשְׁכָּבָהּ בְּשָׁלוֹם. וְנֹאמַר אָמֵן:

❖

Ginsberg's Kaddish, continued

In the world which He[30] has created according to His will Blessed
Praised

Magnified Lauded Exalted the Name of the Holy One Blessed
is He!

In the house in Newark Blessed is He! In the madhouse Blessed
is He! In the house of Death Blessed is He!

Blessed be He in homosexuality! Blessed be He in Paranoia!
Blessed be He in the city! Blessed be He in the Book!

Blessed be He who dwells in the shadow! Blessed Be He!
Blessed be He!

Blessed be you Naomi in tears! Blessed be you Naomi in fears!
Blessed in sickness!

Blessed be you Naomi in Hospitals! Blessed be you Naomi in
solitude! Blest be your triumph! Blest be your bars!
Blest be your last years' loneliness!

Blest be your failure! Blest be your stroke! Blest be the close
of your eye! Blest be the gaunt of your cheek! Blest be
your withered thighs!

Blessed be Thee Naomi in Death! Blessed be Death! Blessed
be death!

Blessed be He Who leads all sorrow to Heaven! Blessed be
He in the end!

Blessed be He who builds Heaven in Darkness! Blessed
Blessed be He! Blessed be He! Blessed be Death on
us All!

Mourners' Kaddish (Recited in Hebrew/Aramaic)

יִתְגַּדַּל וְיִתְקַדַּשׁ שְׁמֵהּ רַבָּא, (עונים: אמן) בְּעָלְמָא דִּי בְרָא כִרְעוּתֵהּ, וְיַמְלִיךְ מַלְכוּתֵהּ בְּחַיֵּיכוֹן וּבְיוֹמֵיכוֹן וּבְחַיֵּי דְּכָל בֵּית יִשְׂרָאֵל, בַּעֲגָלָא וּבִזְמַן קָרִיב, וְאִמְרוּ אָמֵן.

---

[30]We preserved the poet's use of the masculine pronoun for God because the poem functioned, in this liturgy, not as a communal prayer, but as the testimony of an individual.

(וְגֵם הַקָּהָל אוֹמֵר) יְהֵא שְׁמֵהּ רַבָּא מְבָרַךְ לְעָלַם וּלְעָלְמֵי עָלְמַיָּא.

יִתְבָּרַךְ וְיִשְׁתַּבַּח וְיִתְפָּאַר וְיִתְרוֹמַם וְיִתְנַשֵּׂא וְיִתְהַדָּר וְיִתְעַלֶּה וְיִתְהַלָּל

שְׁמֵהּ דְּקֻדְשָׁא בְּרִיךְ הוּא, (עוֹנִים: בְּרִיךְ הוּא) לְעֵלָּא מִן כָּל בִּרְכָתָא /בַּעֲשֶׂרֶת יְמֵי

תְּשׁוּבָה: לְעֵלָּא לְעֵלָּא מִכָּל בִּרְכָתָא/ וְשִׁירָתָא, תֻּשְׁבְּחָתָא וְנֶחֱמָתָא דַּאֲמִירָן

בְּעָלְמָא, וְאִמְרוּ אָמֵן.

יְהֵא שְׁלָמָא רַבָּא מִן שְׁמַיָּא וְחַיִּים עָלֵינוּ וְעַל כָּל יִשְׂרָאֵל, וְאִמְרוּ אָמֵן.

עֹשֶׂה שָׁלוֹם /בַּעֲשֶׂרֶת יְמֵי תְּשׁוּבָה: הַשָּׁלוֹם/ בִּמְרוֹמָיו, הוּא יַעֲשֶׂה שָׁלוֹם עָלֵינוּ

וְעַל כָּל יִשְׂרָאֵל, וְאִמְרוּ אָמֵן.

Recovery . . . is based upon the empowerment of the survivor and the creation of new connections. Recovery can take place only within the context of relationships; it cannot occur in isolation.[31]

Hine Ma Tov (sung in Hebrew)

הִנֵּה מַה־טּוֹב וּמַה־נָּעִים
שֶׁבֶת אַחִים גַּם־יַחַד

---

[31] *WMCH,* p. 286, quoting Judith Lewis Herman, M.D., author of *Trauma and Recovery.*

Havdalah Healing Service*

> *Where:* At synagogue or in a home
>
> *Whom:* Someone recovering from mental illness, his or her family and close friends, caregivers, clergy
>
> *When:* After completion of therapy, upon release from a hospital or treatment center, on a day marking an important event in the course of the illness

Sing meditation of: "Ozi, v'zimrat Yah, va'yehi li, lishu'a"

Hinay, El yishu'ati evtach velo efchad, ki azi vezimrat Yah, Adonai, va'yehi li lishu'a.

Behold, God is my savior, I will trust Him and not be afraid, for my strong faith and song of praise for God will be my salvation. (Isaiah 12:2)

Reading: The *Havdalah* ceremony we are about to perform marks the distinction between the holiness of Shabbat from the rest of the days of the week. Just as we shall mark this distinction, we are here to mark another important moment . . . (Time here for any participant/the central participant to tell a story.)

Sing: La'yehudim ha'yetah orah vesimcha vesason vikar, kayn te'hi'yeh lanu.

The Jews had light, happiness, joy, and honor (Esther 8:16); may we have the same.

Reading: I have been raised from darkness to light, from weakness to strength, and from sickness to health. For all this, for God's help, for all your help and caring, I am grateful. Blessed are You, who constantly renews creation.

Baruch atah, Adonai, Elohaynu melech ha'olam, boray pri hagafen.

Blessed are You, God, our Lord, King of the universe, Creator of the fruit of the vine.

---

*Adapted from CLAL: The National Jewish Center for Learning and Leadership.

Reading: Our Sages teach us that on Shabbat, each one of us is given an extra soul, and that as Shabbat ends, this soul departs from us. We are taught that the smell of the spices each *Havdalah* allows a little bit of that soul to remain with us. So too, on this *Havdalah*, the smell of the spices reminds me that not only is a bit of the extra soul remaining, but too that I was returned to my own soul and life . . .

Baruch atah, Adonai, Elohaynu melech ha'olam, boray minay vesamim.
Blessed are You, God, our Lord, King of the universe, Creator of the different spices.

(Find and insert reading on theme of darkness and light at this point in the service.)

Baruch atah, Adonai, Elohaynu melech ha'olam, boray me'oray ha'aysh.
Blessed are You, God, our Lord, King of the universe, Creator of the fire's lights.

Reading: We take the light of God's presence with us, symbolically, as we move from this place into the streets, from wilderness to promise, from despair to hope. Please take the "light" with you as a reminder of those among us who live with mental illness. Let the light of this candle remind us of the commitment made this day or in days past to be members of a Caring Community for people with mental illness and their families. (Adapted from a Pathways to Promise Interfaith Service.)

Baruch atah, Adonai, Elohaynu melech ha'olam, hamavdil bayn kodesh lechol, bayn or lechoshech, bayn Yisra'el la'amim, bayn yom ha'shevi'i leshayshet yemay hama'aseh. Baruch atah, Adonai, hamavdil bayn kodesh lechol.
Blessed are You, God, our Lord, King of the universe, who separates between the holy and the profane; between the light and dark; between Israel and the other nations; between the seventh day and the six days of the week. Blessed are You, God, who separates between the holy and the profane.

Reading: Each lifetime is the pieces of a jigsaw puzzle.
For some there are more pieces,
For others the puzzle is more difficult to assemble.

Some seem to be born with a nearly completed puzzle.
And so it goes.
Souls trying this way and that
Trying to assemble the myriad parts.

But know this. No one has within themselves
All the pieces to his or her puzzle.
Like before the days they used to seal
jigsaw puzzles in cellophane. Insuring that
all the pieces were there.

Everyone carries with them at least one and probably
Many pieces to someone else's puzzle.

Sometimes they know it.
Sometimes they don't.

And when you present your piece
Which is worthless to you,
to another, whether you know it or not,
Whether they know it or not,
You are a messenger from the Most High.

(Rabbi Lawrence Kushner)

Shavua Tov

Reading (by the central participant): The Talmud teaches us that for surviving four specific events, we are required to give thanks to God. Those who go down into the sea, walk through the deserts, one who was sick and was healed, and one who was jailed and got out, all are to praise God. Rabbi Judith Abrams interprets this passage to mean that illness is metaphorically likened to a dangerous journey or experience wherein one's life is in peril (the high seas and the wilderness) and/or out of one's control (the prisoner). Illness, then, imperils body and soul, effectively keeping us from our true selves.

Baruch atah Adonai, eloheinu melech ha'olam, hagomel le'chayavim tovot, she'gmaliani kol tov.
Blessed are You, Adonai, Sovereign of the universe who graciously bestows favor as favor has been bestowed upon me.

(Response by remaining participants):

Mi she'gmalkha (she'gmalekh) kol tov, hu yigmolkha (yigm'lekh) kol tov selah.
May the One who has been gracious to you continue to favor you with all that is good. Selah.

Part 4

What Is Mental Illness?

The information on the following pages was culled from the website of the National Mental Health Association, at http://www.nmha.org, and is copyrighted and published by the National Mental Health Association. No part of this document may be reproduced without written consent. In addition to these fact sheets, the website has many others.

Before even beginning to address mental illness and the mentally ill in our congregations, we must be equipped with a general base of information about mental illness. The following pages describe myths and realities about mental illness. All too often, unfortunately, the myth is more familiar to us than the reality. This section is designed to provide an overview of mental illness—what it is, common manifestations in the community, important terms, and warning signs.

Depression

Clinical depression is a common, real, and treatable illness.

Basic Facts about Clinical Depression

- Clinical depression is one of the most common mental illnesses, affecting more than nineteen million Americans each year.[1] This includes major depressive disorder, manic depression, and dysthymia, a milder, longer-lasting form of depression.
- Depression causes people to lose pleasure from daily life, can complicate other medical conditions, and can even be serious enough to lead to suicide.
- Depression can occur to anyone, at any age, and to people of any race or ethnic group.
- Depression is never a "normal" part of life, no matter what your age, gender, or health situation.
- Unfortunately, though treatment for depression is almost always successful, fewer than half of those suffering from this illness seek treatment.[2] Too many people resist treatment because they believe depression isn't serious, that they can treat it themselves, or that it is a personal weakness rather than a serious medical illness.

Treatments for Clinical Depression

Clinical depression is very treatable, with more than 80 percent of those who seek treatment showing improvement.[3] The most commonly used treatments are antidepressant medication, psychotherapy, or a combination of the two. The choice of treatment depends on the pattern, severity, and persistence of depressive symptoms, and the history of the illness. As with many illnesses, early treatment is more effective and helps prevent the likelihood of serious recurrences. Depression must be treated by a physician or qualified mental health professional.

---

[1]National Institute of Mental Health, "The Numbers Count: Mental Illness in America," *Science on Our Minds Fact Sheet Series.* Accessed August 1999. http://www.nimh.nih.gov/publicat/numbers.cfm.
[2]A. Rupp, E. Gause, and D. Regier, "Research Policy Implications of Cost-of-Illness Studies for Mental Disorders," *British Journal of Psychiatry Suppl.* (1998), 36:19–25.
[3]Ibid.

Symptoms of Clinical Depression

- Persistent sad, anxious, or "empty" mood
- Sleeping too much or too little, middle of the night or early morning waking
- Reduced appetite and weight loss or increased appetite and weight gain
- Loss of pleasure and interest in activities once enjoyed, including sex
- Restlessness, irritability
- Persistent physical symptoms that do not respond to treatment (such as chronic pain or digestive disorders)
- Difficulty concentrating, remembering, or making decisions
- Fatigue or loss of energy
- Feeling guilty, hopeless, or worthless
- Thoughts of suicide or death

If you have five or more of these symptoms for two weeks or more, you could have clinical depression and should see your doctor or a qualified mental health professional for help.

Causes of Clinical Depression

Many things can contribute to clinical depression. For some people, a number of factors seem to be involved, while for others a single factor can cause the illness. Oftentimes, people become depressed for no apparent reason.

- Biological—People with depression typically have too little or too much of certain brain chemicals, called "neurotransmitters." Changes in these brain chemicals may cause or contribute to clinical depression.
- Cognitive—People with negative thinking patterns and low self-esteem are more likely to develop clinical depression.
- Gender—Women experience clinical depression at a rate that is nearly twice that of men.[4] While the reasons for this are still unclear, they may include the hormonal changes women go through during menstruation, pregnancy, childbirth, and menopause. Other reasons may include the stress caused by the multiple responsibilities that women have.
- Co-occurrence—Clinical depression is more likely to occur along with certain illnesses, such as heart disease, cancer, Parkinson's disease, diabetes, Alzheimer's disease, and hormonal disorders.
- Medications—Side effects of some medications can bring about depression.
- Genetic—A family history of clinical depression increases the risk for developing the illness.
- Situational—Difficult life events, including divorce, financial problems, or the death of a loved one can contribute to clinical depression.

---

[4]National Institute of Mental Health, D/ART Campaign, "Depression: What Every Woman Should Know" (1995), Pub No. 95-3871.

Bipolar Disorder

What Is Bipolar Disorder?

Bipolar disorder, also known as manic depression, is an illness involving one or more episodes of serious mania and depression. The illness causes a person's mood to swing from excessively "high" and/or irritable to sad and hopeless, with periods of a normal mood in between. More than two million Americans suffer from bipolar disorder.

Bipolar disorder typically begins in adolescence or early adulthood and continues throughout life. It is often not recognized as an illness and people who have it may suffer needlessly for years.

Bipolar disorder can be extremely distressing and disruptive for those who have this disease, their spouses, family members, friends, and employers. Although there is no known cure, bipolar disorder is treatable, and recovery is possible. Individuals with bipolar disorder have successful relationships and meaningful jobs. The combination of medications and psychotherapy helps the vast majority of people return to productive, fulfilling lives.

What Causes Bipolar Disorder?

Although a specific genetic link to bipolar disorder has not been found, studies show that 80 to 90 percent of those who suffer from bipolar disorder have relatives with some form of depression.

It is also possible that people may inherit a *tendency to develop* the illness, which can then be triggered by environmental factors such as distressing life events.

The presence of bipolar disorder indicates a biochemical imbalance that alters a person's moods. This imbalance is thought to be caused by irregular hormone production or a problem with certain chemicals in the brain, called neurotransmitters, that act as messengers to our nerve cells.

What Are the Symptoms of Bipolar Disorder?

Bipolar disorder is often difficult to recognize and diagnose. It causes a person to have a high level of energy, unrealistically expansive thoughts or ideas, and impulsive or reckless behavior. These symptoms may feel good to a person, which may lead to denial that there is a problem.

Another reason bipolar disorder is difficult to diagnose is that its symptoms may appear to be part of another illness or may be attributed to other problems such as substance abuse, poor school performance, or trouble in the workplace.

Symptoms of Mania

Listed below are symptoms of mania, which can last up to three months if untreated.

- Excessive energy, activity, restlessness, racing thoughts, and rapid talking.
- Denial that anything is wrong.
- Extreme "high" or euphoric feelings—a person may feel "on top of the world" and nothing, including bad news or tragic events, can change this "happiness."
- Frequent irritation or distraction.
- Decreased need for sleep—an individual may last for days with little or no sleep without feeling tired.
- Unrealistic beliefs in one's ability and powers—a person may experience feelings of exaggerated confidence or unwarranted optimism. This can lead to overambitious work plans and the belief that nothing can stop him or her from accomplishing any task.
- Uncharacteristically poor judgment—a person may make poor decisions, which may lead to unrealistic involvement in activities, meetings, and deadlines, reckless driving, spending sprees, and foolish business ventures.
- Sustained period of behavior that is different from usual—a person may dress and/or act differently than he or she usually does, become a collector of various items, become indifferent to personal grooming, become obsessed with writing, or experience delusions.
- Unusual sexual drive.
- Abuse of drugs, particularly cocaine, alcohol, or sleeping medications.
- Provocative, intrusive, or aggressive behavior—a person may become enraged or paranoid if his or her grand ideas are stopped or excessive social plans are refused.

Symptoms of Depression

Some people experience periods of normal mood and behavior following a manic phase; however, the depressive phase will eventually appear. Symptoms of depression are listed on page 66.

Treatment of Bipolar Disorder

Treatment is critical for recovery. A combination of medication, professional help, and support from family, friends, and peers helps individuals with bipolar disorder stabilize their emotions and behavior.

Most people with bipolar disorder can be treated with medication. A common medication, Lithium, is effective in controlling mania in 60 percent of individuals with bipolar disorder. Olanzapine (Zyprexa), an antipsychotic, is a new treatment for bipolar disorder.

Carbomazepine (Tegratol) and divalproex sodium (Depakote), which are mood-stabilizers and anticonvulsants, are some of the other medications used. In addition, benzodiazepines are sometimes prescribed for insomnia, and thyroid medication can also be helpful.

It is suggested that those with bipolar disorder receive guidance, education, and support from a mental health professional to help deal with personal relationships, maintain a healthy self-image, and ensure compliance with treatment.

Support and self-help groups are also an invaluable resource for learning coping skills, feeling acceptance, and avoiding social isolation. Friends and family should join a support group to better understand the illness so that they can continue to offer encouragement and support to their loves ones.

Sources

"Bipolar Disorder," NIMH, U.S. Department of Health and Human Services.
"Facts About: Manic Depression," American Psychiatric Association.
"Overview of Bipolar Disorder and Its Symptoms," National Depressive and Manic Depressive Association.

Schizophrenia

Schizophrenia is a serious disorder that affects how a person thinks, feels, and acts. Someone with schizophrenia may have difficulty distinguishing between what is real and what is imaginary, may be unresponsive or withdrawn, and may have difficulty expressing normal emotions in social situations.

Contrary to public perception, schizophrenia is *not* split personality or multiple personality. The vast majority of people with schizophrenia are *not* violent and do not pose a danger to others. Schizophrenia is *not* caused by childhood experiences, poor parenting, or lack of willpower, nor are the symptoms identical for each person.

Schizophrenia affects about 1 percent of the world population. In the United States one in a hundred people, about 2.5 million, have this disease. It knows no racial, cultural, or economic boundaries. Symptoms usually appear between the ages of thirteen and twenty-five, but often appear earlier in males than females.

No cure for schizophrenia has been discovered, but with proper treatment, many people with this illness can lead productive and fulfilling lives.

What Causes Schizophrenia?

The cause of schizophrenia is still unclear. Some theories about the cause of this disease include genetics (heredity), biology (the imbalance in the brain's chemistry), and/or possible viral infections and immune disorders.

Scientists recognize that the disorder tends to run in families and that a person inherits a tendency to develop the disease. Schizophrenia may also be triggered by environmental events, such as viral infections or highly stressful situations or a combination of both.

Similar to some other genetically related illnesses, schizophrenia appears when the body undergoes hormonal and physical changes, like those that occur during puberty in the teen and young adult years.

Genetics help to determine how the brain uses certain chemicals. People with schizophrenia have a chemical imbalance of serotonin and dopamine, which are neurotransmitters. These neurotransmitters allow nerve cells in the brain to send messages to each other. The imbalance of these chemicals affects the way a person's brain reacts to stimuli, which explains why a person with schizophrenia may be overwhelmed by sensory information (loud music or bright lights) that other people can easily handle. This problem in processing different sounds, sights, smells, and tastes can also lead to hallucinations or delusions.

What Are the Early Warning Signs of Schizophrenia?

The signs of schizophrenia are different for everyone. Symptoms may develop slowly over months or years, or may appear very abruptly. The disease may come and go in cycles of relapse and remission. Behaviors that are early warning signs of schizophrenia include:

- Hearing or seeing something that isn't there
- A constant feeling of being watched
- A peculiar or nonsensical way of speaking or writing
- Strange body positioning
- Feeling indifferent to very important situations
- Deterioration of academic or work performance
- A change in personal hygiene and appearance
- A change in personality
- Increasing withdrawal from social situations
- Irrational, angry, or fearful response to loved ones
- Inability to sleep or concentrate
- Inappropriate or bizarre behavior
- Extreme preoccupation with religion or the occult

If you or a loved one experience several of these symptoms for more than two weeks, seek help immediately.

What Are the Symptoms of Schizophrenia?

A medical or mental health professional may use the following terms when discussing the symptoms of schizophrenia.

Positive symptoms are disturbances that are "added" to the person's personality.

- Delusions—individuals may believe that someone is spying on them or that they are someone famous.
- Hallucinations—seeing, feeling, tasting, hearing, or smelling something that doesn't really exist. The most common experience is hearing imaginary voices that give commands or comments to the individual.
- Disordered thinking and speech—moving from one topic to another in a nonsensical fashion. Individuals may make up their own words or sounds.

Negative symptoms are capabilities that are "lost" from the person's personality.

- Social withdrawal
- Extreme apathy
- Lack of drive or initiative
- Emotional unresponsiveness

What Are the Different Types of Schizophrenia?

- Paranoid schizophrenia—a person feels extremely suspicious, persecuted, or grandiose, or experiences a combination of these emotions.

- Disorganized schizophrenia—a person is often incoherent in speech and thought, but may not have delusions.
- Catatonic schizophrenia—a person is withdrawn, mute, negative, and often assumes very unusual body positions.
- Residual schizophrenia—a person is no longer experiencing delusions or hallucinations, but has no motivation or interest in life.
- Schizoaffective disorder—a person has symptoms of both schizophrenia and a major mood disorder such as depression.

What Treatments Are Available for Schizophrenia?

If you suspect someone you know is experiencing symptoms of schizophrenia, encourage him or her to see a medical or mental health professional immediately. Early treatment—even as early as the first episode—can mean a better long-term outcome.

While no cure for schizophrenia exists, many people with this illness can lead productive and fulfilling lives with the proper treatment. Recovery is possible through a variety of services, including rehabilitation programs and medication. Rehabilitation can help a person recover the confidence and skills needed to live a productive and independent life in the community. Types of services that help a person with schizophrenia are listed below.

- Case management helps people access services, financial assistance, treatment, and other resources.
- Psychosocial rehabilitation programs are programs that help people regain skills such as employment, cooking, cleaning, budgeting, shopping, socializing, problem solving, and stress management.
- Self-help groups provide ongoing support and information to persons with serious mental illness by individuals who experience mental illness themselves.
- Drop-in centers are places where individuals with mental illness can socialize and/or receive informal support and services on an as-needed basis.
- Housing programs offer a range of support and supervision from twenty-four-hour supervised living to drop-in support as needed.
- Employment programs assist individuals in finding employment and/or gaining the skills necessary to re-enter the workforce.
- Therapy/counseling includes different forms of "talk" therapy, both individual and group, that can help both the patient and family members to better understand the illness and share their concerns.
- Crisis services include twenty-four-hour hotlines, after hours counseling, residential placement, and in-patient hospitalization.

The new generation of antipsychotic medications help people with schizophrenia to live fulfilling lives. They help to reduce the biochemical imbalances that cause schizophrenia and decrease the likelihood of relapse. Like all medications, however, antipsychotic medications should be taken only under the supervision of a mental health professional. There are two major types of antipsychotic medication.

- Conventional antipsychotics effectively control the "positive" symptoms such as the hallucinations, delusions, and confusion of schizophrenia.

- New generation (also called atypical) antipsychotics treat both the positive and negative symptoms of schizophrenia, often with fewer side effects.

Side effects are common with antipsychotic drugs. They range from mild side effects such as dry mouth, blurred vision, constipation, drowsiness, and dizziness, which usually disappear after a few weeks, to more serious side effects such as trouble with muscle control, pacing, tremors, and facial ticks. The newer generation of drugs have fewer side effects. However, it is important to talk with your mental health professional before making any changes in medication since many side effects can be controlled.

Anxiety Disorders*

Generalized Anxiety Disorder

Generalized Anxiety Disorder (GAD) is characterized by six months or more of chronic, exaggerated worry and tension that is unfounded or much more severe than the normal anxiety most people experience. People with this disorder usually expect the worst; they worry excessively about money, health, family, or work, even when there are no signs of trouble. They are unable to relax and often suffer from insomnia. Many people with GAD also have physical symptoms, such as fatigue, trembling, muscle tension, headaches, irritability, or hot flashes.

Fortunately, through research supported by the National Institute of Mental Health (NIMH), effective treatments have been developed to help people with GAD.

How Common Is GAD?

- About 2.8 percent of the U.S. population (four million Americans) have GAD during a year's time.
- GAD most often strikes people in childhood or adolescence, but can begin in adulthood, too. It affects women more often than men.

What Causes GAD?

Some research suggests that GAD may run in families and it may also grow worse during stress. GAD usually begins at an earlier age and symptoms may manifest themselves more slowly than in most other anxiety disorders.

What Treatments Are Available for GAD?

Treatments for GAD include medications and cognitive-behavioral therapy.

---

*The contents of the fact sheets on anxiety disorders were adapted from material published by the National Institute of Mental Health.

Can People with GAD Also Have Other Physical and Emotional Illnesses?

Research shows that GAD often coexists with depression, substance abuse, or other anxiety disorders. Other conditions associated with stress, such as irritable bowel syndrome, often accompany GAD. Patients with physical symptoms such as insomnia or headaches should also tell their doctors about their feelings of worry and tension. This will help the patient's health care provider to recognize that the person is suffering from GAD.

Panic Disorder

Panic disorder is characterized by unexpected and repeated episodes of intense fear accompanied by physical symptoms that may include chest pain, heart palpitations, shortness of breath, dizziness, or abdominal distress. These sensations often mimic symptoms of a heart attack or other life-threatening medical conditions. As a result, the diagnosis of panic disorder is frequently not made until extensive and costly medical procedures fail to provide a correct diagnosis or relief.

Many people with panic disorder develop intense anxiety between episodes, worrying when and where the next one will strike. Fortunately, through research supported by the National Institute of Mental Health (NIMH), effective treatments have been developed to help people with panic disorder.

How Common Is Panic Disorder?

- In a given year 1.7 percent of the U.S. population (2.4 million Americans) experiences panic disorder.
- Women are twice as likely as men to develop panic disorder.
- Panic disorder typically strikes in young adulthood. Roughly half of all people who have panic disorder develop the condition before age twenty-four.

What Causes Panic Disorder?

Heredity, other biological factors, stressful life events, and thinking in a way that exaggerates relatively normal bodily reactions in catastrophic events are all believed to play a role in the onset of panic disorder. Some research suggests panic attacks occur when a "suffocation alarm mechanism" in the brain erroneously fires, falsely reporting that death is imminent. The exact cause or causes of panic disorder are unknown and are the subject of intense scientific investigation.

What Treatments Are Available for Panic Disorder?

Treatment for panic disorder includes medications and a type of psychotherapy known as cognitive-behavioral therapy, which teaches people how to view panic attacks differently and demonstrates ways to reduce anxiety. NIMH is conducting a large-scale study to evaluate the effectiveness of combining these treatments. Appropriate treatment by an experienced professional can reduce or prevent panic attacks in 70 to 90 percent of people with panic disorder. Most patients show significant progress after a few weeks of therapy. Relapses may occur, but they can often be effectively treated just like the initial episode.

Can People with Panic Disorder Also Have Other Physical and Emotional Illnesses?

Research shows that panic disorder can coexist with other disorders, most often depression and substance abuse. About 30 percent of people with panic disorder use alcohol and 17 percent use drugs, such as cocaine and marijuana, in unsuccessful attempts to alleviate the anguish and distress caused by their condition. Appropriate diagnosis and treatment of other disorders, such as substance abuse or depression, are important to the successful treatment of panic disorder. Approximately 20 percent of people with panic disorder attempt suicide.

It is not unusual for a person with panic disorder to develop phobias about places or situations where panic attacks have occurred, such as in supermarkets or other everyday locations. As the frequency of panic attacks increases, the person often begins to avoid situations where he or she fears another attack may occur or where help would not be immediately available. This avoidance may eventually develop into agoraphobia, an inability to go beyond known and safe surroundings because of intense fear and anxiety.

People with panic disorder may also have irritable bowel syndrome, characterized by intermittent bouts of gastrointestinal cramps and diarrhea or constipation, or a relatively minor heart problem called mitral valve prolapse. In fact, panic disorder often coexists with unexplained medical problems, such as chest pain not associated with a heart attack or chronic fatigue.

Obsessive-Compulsive Disorder

People with obsessive-compulsive disorder (OCD) suffer intensely from recurrent unwanted thoughts (obsessions) or rituals (compulsions), which they feel they cannot control. Rituals such as handwashing, counting, checking, or cleaning are often performed in hope of preventing obsessive thoughts or making them go away. Performing these rituals, however, provides only temporary relief, and not performing them markedly increases anxiety. Left untreated, obsessions and the need to perform rituals can take over a person's life. OCD is often a chronic, relapsing illness.

Fortunately, through research supported by the National Institute of Mental Health (NIMH), effective treatments have been developed to help people with OCD.

How Common Is OCD?

- About 2.3 percent of the U.S. population (3.3 million Americans) experiences OCD in a given year.
- OCD affects men and women equally.
- OCD typically begins during adolescence or early childhood; at least one-third of the cases of adult OCD began in childhood.
- OCD cost the U.S. $8.4 billion in 1990 in social and economic losses, nearly 6 percent of the total mental health bill of $148 billion.

What Causes OCD?

There is growing evidence that OCD has a neurobiological basis. OCD is no longer attributed to family problems or to attitudes learned in childhood—for example, an inordinate emphasis on cleanliness, or a belief that certain thoughts are dangerous or unacceptable. Instead, the search for causes now focuses on the interaction between neurobiological factors and environmental influences. Brain imaging studies using a technique called positron emission tomography (PET) have compared people with and without OCD. Those with OCD have patterns of brain activity that differ from those of people with other mental illnesses or with no mental illness at all. In addition, PET scans show that in patients with OCD, both behavioral therapy and medication produce changes in the caudate nucleus, a part of the brain. This is graphic evidence that both psychotherapy and medication affect the brain.

What Treatments Are Available for OCD?

Treatments for OCD have been developed through research supported by the NIMH and other research institutions. These treatments, which combine medications and behavioral therapy (a specific type of psychotherapy), are often effective.

Several medications have been proven effective in helping people with OCD: clomipramine, fluoxetine, fluvoxamine, and paroxetine. If one drug is not effective, others should be tried. A number of other medications are currently being studied.

A type of behavioral therapy known as "exposure and response prevention" is very useful for treating OCD. In this approach, a person is deliberately and voluntarily exposed to whatever triggers the obsessive thoughts and then is taught techniques to avoid performing the compulsive rituals and to deal with the anxiety.

Can People with OCD Also Have Other Physical or Emotional Illnesses?

OCD is sometimes accompanied by depression, eating disorders, substance abuse, attention deficit hyperactivity disorder, or other anxiety disorders. When a person also has other disorders, OCD is often more difficult to diagnose and treat. Symptoms of OCD can also coexist and may even be part of a spectrum of neurological disorders, such as Tourette's syndrome. Appropriate diagnosis and treatment of other disorders is important to successful treatment of OCD.

Phobias

Everyone feels anxious or uneasy from time to time. Your first day on a new job, planning for a long trip, going to the dentist—your palms sweat, you feel shaky, your heart pounds. Some anxiety helps to keep you focused on the job at hand. However, when your anxiety is so serious that it interferes with your work, leads you to avoid certain situations, or keeps you from enjoying life, you may be suffering from a phobia, a form of the most common type of mental disorder, an anxiety disorder.

Anxiety disorders are not just a case of "nerves." You can't overcome an anxiety disorder just through willpower, nor can the symptoms be ignored or wished away. These disorders cause you to feel anxious most of the time, making some everyday situations so uncomfortable that you may avoid them entirely. Or, you may experience occasional instances of anxiety that are so terrifying and intense that you may be immobilized with fear.

Although these conditions can be very frightening and disabling, they are also very treatable. It is important to recognize the symptoms and seek help.

Specifically, phobias afflict as many as 12 percent of all Americans. They are the most common psychiatric illness in women and the second most common in men over age twenty-five. Phobias are not all the same. There are three main groups, which include:

- Specific (simple) phobias, which are the most common and focus on specific objects,
- Social phobia, which causes extreme anxiety in social or public situations, and
- Agoraphobia, which is the fear of being alone in public places from which there is no easy escape.

Agoraphobia causes people to suffer anxiety about being in places or situations from which it might be difficult or embarrassing to escape, such as being in a room full of people or in an elevator. In some cases, panic attacks can become so debilitating that the person may develop agoraphobia because he or she fears another panic attack. In extreme cases, a person with agoraphobia may be afraid to leave his or her house.

Specific or simple phobias produce intense fear of a particular object or situation that is, in fact, relatively safe. People who suffer from specific phobias are aware that their fear is irrational, but the thought of facing the object or situation often brings on a panic attack or severe anxiety.

Specific phobias strike more than one in ten people. No one knows what causes them, though they seem to run in families and are slightly more prevelant in women. Specific phobias usually begin in adolescence or adulthood. They start suddenly and tend to be more persistent than childhood phobias; only about 20 percent of adult phobias vanish on their own. When children have specific phobias—for example, a fear of animals—those fears usually disappear over time, though they may continue into adulthood. No one knows why they persist in some people and disappear in others.

Examples of specific phobias include persistent fear of dogs, insects, or snakes; driving a car; heights; tunnels or bridges; thunderstorms; and flying.

Social phobia can produce fear of being humiliated or embarrassed in front of other people. This problem may also be related to feelings of inferiority and low self-esteem, and can drive a person to drop out of school, avoid making friends, and remain unemployed.

Although this disorder is sometimes thought to be shyness, it is not the same thing. Shy people do not experience extreme anxiety in social situations, nor do they necessarily avoid them. In contrast, people with social phobia can be at ease with people most of the time, except in particular situations. Often social phobia is accompanied by depression or substance abuse.

People suffering from social phobia may

- View small mistakes as more exaggerated than they really are
- Find blushing to be painfully embarrassing
- Feel that all eyes are on them
- Fear speaking in public, dating, or talking with persons in authority
- Fear using public restrooms or eating out
- Fear talking on the phone or writing in front of others

There is hope for people with phobias.

- No one should have to endure the terror of phobias or the unrelenting anticipatory anxiety that often accompanies them. Phobias can be overcome with proper treatment.

- A person suffering from a phobia is suffering from a diagnosable illness, and mental health professionals take this illness very seriously.
- A complete medical and psychiatric evaluation should be conducted by a licensed physician or psychologist to obtain an accurate diagnosis and ensure that the symptoms are not being caused by another condition.
- It is crucial to comply with treatment, and to work closely with the therapist in order to achieve success.
- Behavioral therapy and cognitive-behavioral therapy are very effective in treating these disorders.
    - *Behavioral therapy* focuses on changing specific actions and uses different techniques to stop the behavior. One technique involves *diaphragmatic breathing,* which is a form of deep-breathing. Another technique called *exposure therapy* gradually exposes the patient to the object or situation that frightens him or her and helps the patient to develop coping skills.
    - *Cognitive-behavioral therapy* teaches the person new skills in order to react differently to the situations that trigger the anxiety or panic attacks. Patients also learn to understand how their thinking patterns contribute to the symptoms and how to change their thinking to reduce or stop these symptoms.

Post-Traumatic Stress Disorder

Post-traumatic stress disorder (PTSD) is an extremely debilitating condition that can occur after exposure to a terrifying event or ordeal in which grave physical harm occurred or was threatened. Traumatic events that can trigger PTSD include violent personal assaults such as rape or mugging, natural or human-caused disasters and accidents, and military combat.

Military troops who served in Vietnam and the Gulf Wars; rescue workers involved in the aftermath of the Oklahoma City Bombing; survivors of accidents, rape, physical and sexual abuse, and other crimes; immigrants fleeing violence in their countries; survivors of the 1994 California earthquake, the 1997 South Dakota floods, and hurricanes Hugo and Andrew, and the events of 9/11/01; and people who witness traumatic events are among the people who develop PTSD. Families of victims can also develop the disorder.

Fortunately, through research supported by the National Institute of Mental Health (NIMH) and the Department of Veterans Affairs (VA), effective treatments have been developed to help people with PTSD. Research is also helping scientists better understand the condition and how it affects the brain and the rest of the body.

What Are the Symptoms of PTSD?

Many people with PTSD repeatedly re-experience the ordeal in the form of flashback episodes, memories, nightmares, or frightening thoughts, especially when they are exposed to events or objects reminiscent of the trauma. Anniversaries of the event can also trigger symptoms. People with PTSD also experience emotional numbness and sleep disturbances, depression, anxiety, and irritability or outbursts of anger. Feelings of intense guilt are also common. Most people with PTSD try to avoid any reminders or thoughts of the ordeal. PTSD is diagnosed when symptoms last more than one month.

How Common Is PTSD?

At least 3.6 percent of U.S. adults (5.2 million Americans) have PTSD during the course of a year. About 30 percent of the men and women who have spent time in war zones experience PTSD. One million war veterans developed PTSD after serving in Vietnam. PTSD has also been detected among veterans of the Persian Gulf War, with some estimates running as high as 8 percent.

When Does PTSD First Occur?

PTSD can develop at any age, including in childhood. Symptoms typically begin within three months of a traumatic event, although occasionally they do not begin until years later. Once PTSD occurs, the severity and duration of the illness varies. Some people recover within six months, while others suffer much longer.

What Treatments Are Available for PTSD?

Research has demonstrated the effectiveness of cognitive-behavioral therapy, group therapy, and exposure therapy, in which the patient repeatedly relives the frightening experience under controlled conditions to help him or her work through the trauma. Medications have also been shown to help ease the symptoms of depression and anxiety and help promote sleep. Scientists are attempting to determine which treatments work best for which type of trauma.

Do Other Physical or Emotional Illnesses Tend to Accompany PTSD?

Depression, alcohol or other substance abuse, or anxiety disorders are not uncommon co-occurrences for people with PTSD. The likelihood of treatment success is increased when these other conditions are appropriately diagnosed and treated as well.

Headaches, gastrointestinal complaints, immune system problems, dizziness, chest pain, or discomfort in other parts of the body are also common. Often, doctors treat the symptoms without being aware that they stem from PTSD. NIMH, through its education program, is encouraging primary care providers to ask patients about experiences with violence, recent losses, and traumatic events, especially if symptoms are recurring. When PTSD is diagnosed, referral to a mental health professional who has had experience treating people with the disorder is recommended.

Who Is Most Likely to Develop PTSD?

People who have been abused as children or who have had other previous traumatic experiences are more likely to develop the disorder. Research is continuing to pinpoint other factors that may lead to PTSD.

What Are Scientists Learning from Research?

NIMH and the VA sponsor a wide range of basic, clinical, and genetic studies of PTSD. In addition, NIMH has a special funding mechanism, called RAPID Grants, which allows researchers to visit immediately the scenes of disasters, such as plane crashes or floods and hurricanes, to study the acute effects of the event and the effectiveness of early intervention.

Research has shown that PTSD clearly alters a number of fundamental brain mechanisms. Because of this, abnormalities have been detected in brain chemicals that mediate coping behavior, learning, and memory among people with the disorder. Recent brain imaging studies have detected altered metabolism and blood flow as well as anatomical changes in people with PTSD.

The following are also recent research findings:

- Some studies show that debriefing people very soon after a catastrophic event may reduce some of the symptoms of PTSD. A study of twelve thousand school children who lived through a hurricane in Hawaii found that those who got counseling early on were doing much better two years later than those who did not.
- People with PTSD tend to have abnormal levels of key hormones involved in response to stress. Cortisol levels are lower than normal and epinephrine and norepinephrine are higher than normal. Scientists have also found that people with this condition have alterations in the function of the thyroid and in neurotransmitter activity involving serotonin and opiates.
- When people are in danger, they produce high levels of natural opiates, which can temporarily mask pain. Scientists have found that people with PTSD continue to produce those higher levels even after the danger has passed; this may lead to the blunted emotions associated with the condition.
- It used to be believed that people who tend to dissociate themselves from a trauma were showing a healthy response, but now some researchers suspect that people who experience dissociation may be more prone to PTSD.
- Animal studies show that the hippocampus—a part of the brain critical to emotion-laden memories—appears to be smaller in cases of PTSD. Brain imaging studies indicate similar findings in humans. Scientists are investigating whether this is related to short-term memory problems. Changes in the hippocampus are thought to be responsible for intrusive memories and flashbacks that occur in people with this disorder.
- Research to understand the neurotransmitter system involved in memories of emotionally charged events may lead to the discovery of drugs that, if given early, could block the development of PTSD symptoms.
- Levels of CRF, or corticotropin releasing factor—the ignition switch in the human stress response—seem to be elevated in people with PTSD, which may account for the tendency to be easily startled. Because of this finding, scientists now want to determine whether drugs that reduce CRF activity are useful in treating the disorder.

Alzheimer's Disease

Alzheimer's disease (AD) is the most common cause of dementia in older people. A dementia is a medical condition that disrupts the way the brain works. AD affects the parts of the brain that control thought, memory, and language. Although the risk of getting the disease increases with age, it is not a normal part of aging. At present the cause of the disease is unknown and there is no cure.

AD is named after Dr. Alois Alzheimer, a German psychiatrist. In 1906, Dr. Alzheimer described changes in the brain tissue of a woman who had died of an unusual mental illness. He found abnormal deposits (now called senile or neuritic plaques) and tangled bundles of nerve fibers (now called neurofibrillary tangles). These plaques and tangles in the brain have come to be characteristic brain changes owing to AD.

It is estimated that currently four million people in the United States may have Alzheimer's disease. The disease usually begins after age sixty-five and risk of AD goes up with age. While younger people may have AD, it is much less common. About 3 percent of men and women ages sixty-five to seventy-four have AD and nearly half of those over age eighty-five could have the disease.

Symptoms include:

- Initial mild forgetfulness
- Confusion with names and simple mathematical problems
- Forgetfulness to do simple everyday tasks, i.e., brushing one's teeth
- Problems speaking, understanding, reading, and writing
- Behavioral and personality changes
- Aggressive, anxious, or aimless behavior

Diagnosis

No definitive test to diagnose Alzheimer's disease in living patients exists. However, in specialized research facilities, neurologists now can diagnose AD with up to 90 percent accuracy. The following is some of the information used to make this diagnosis:

- A complete medical history
- Basic medical tests (i.e., blood, urine tests)
- Neuropsychological tests (i.e., memory, problem-solving, language tests)
- Brain scans (i.e., MRI scan, CT scan, or PET scan)

Research for Possible Risk Factors

Scientists are trying to learn what causes AD and how to prevent it. This list may not be all inclusive or definitive. However, research has lead scientists to consider the following as possible risk factors:

- Genetics.
- Environment—aluminum, zinc, and other metals have been detected in the brain tissue of those with AD. However, it isn't known whether they cause AD, or build up in the brain as a result of AD.
- Viruses—viruses that might cause the changes seen in the brain tissue of AD patients are being studied.

The only known risk factors are age and family history. Serious head injury and lower levels of education may also be risk factors. AD is probably not caused by any one factor. Most likely, it is caused by several factors together that react differently in each person. Unfortunately, no blood or urine test currently exists that can detect or predict AD.

Treatment of Alzheimer's Disease

Alzheimer's disease advances in stages, ranging from mild forgetfulness to severe dementia. The course of the disease and the rate of decline varies from person to person. The duration from onset of symptoms to death can be from five to twenty years.

Currently, there is no effective treatment for AD that can halt the progression. However, some experimental drugs have shown promise in easing symptoms in some patients. Medications can help control behavioral symptoms, making patients more comfortable and easier to manage for caregivers. Still other research efforts focus on alternative care programs that provide relief to the caregiver and support for the patient.

Dual Diagnosis

It is generally agreed in the world of psychiatry that as much as 50 percent of the mentally ill population also has a substance abuse problem. This combination is known as a dual diagnosis, and it makes both of the problems more difficult to treat. Despite the common incidence of dual diagnosis, many mental health services are not prepared to deal with patients who have both afflictions. Often, only one is recognized; if both are diagnosed, the individual may bounce back and forth between treatments for the mental illness and those for substance abuse, or worse, be refused treatment for both.

Part 5

What Can Congregations Do to Help the Mentally Ill and Their Families?

Our texts tell the story of when Rabbi Yochanan fell ill, and Rabbi Hanina went to visit him. Rabbi Hanina asked, "Are your sufferings welcome to you?" Rabbi Yochanan answered, "Neither they nor their reward." So Rabbi Hanina said, "Give me your hand." Rabbi Yochanan reached up his hand, and Rabbi Hanina raised him. The text asks, "Why could not Rabbi Yochanan raise himself?" It answered, "The prisoner cannot free himself from jail" (Talmud Bavli, *B'rachot* 5b).

Of the many lessons on healing and illness we can learn from this text, perhaps one of the most important is the one of reaching out. In the story, it is a physical act of raising the sick. In our lives, it can be any act from a personal phone call to a mentally ill congregant, to opening the congregation to a community-wide conference on mental health, to starting a support group for mentally ill congregants and/or their family members.

This section, on what your congregation can do, covers all of these possibilities and more. In addition to the information found here, the Department of Jewish Family Concerns at the UAHC has brochures, programs, and program suggestions.

Like any new project or initiative, immediate action cannot be expected on the part of the congregation. And given the sensitivities surrounding this topic in general, any activity is likely to come about only as the product of a change process. As professionals, we must strive to create awareness as the first step. Once there is a general awareness in the community of the need for a new program, we begin a process of teaching, of giving the community the knowledge it needs for the final step of this process. In the final step, we join our communities in taking action, such as those outlined in this section and others.

Getting Started

Programming can be focused solely on one population, such as those who have a mental illness, or it can address a variety of needs, including those of a mentally ill population. The choice of program should fit the "art of the possible" in each synagogue's situation. If a program focusing solely on mental illness is not feasible in your situation, make the choice to address mental illness via programs that include the issue along with others. The important thing is to make an effort to meet the needs of the mentally ill and their families, a population whose needs, until now, have largely been overlooked by the synagogue.

The support of the rabbi in any congregational undertaking is critical. The rabbi's input, direction, and support is most important in presenting an image of purpose. The rabbi has a particularly crucial role when a program deals with illness and grief. The rabbi may not have occasion to give much attention to mental illness. Ascertain how the rabbi views this issue.

Also, one cannot overemphasize the importance of a well-developed program of volunteer training. Many different styles of training exist and may vary as to size and resources available. Keep in mind that in addition to specialists who may be available within the congregation, outside resources from communal agencies such as the Jewish Federation, Jewish Family and Children Services, Jewish Vocational Services, and the local mental health center or office of the Department of Health, may be invaluable help in developing and implementing volunteer training. This training is vital as is follow-up support to ensure that the needs of congregants are being met and to provide advance warning of volunteer burnout.

Successful volunteer involvement is based on respect, understanding, and trust. A synagogue (or Jewish communal service agency) and its paid staff must be willing, and be trained, to work with volunteers. Staff must develop an appreciation for the roll of the volunteer as a person who can relate to program participants in a nonclinical manner.

The following is a step-by-step list of the actions a congregation should take when developing a program or programs addressing the needs of the mentally ill.

I. Organize a focus group or task force.
    A. Identify and convene members of the congregation who have personal concern and knowledge about the need you are going to address, including mental illness.
    B. Identify persons who have a need for this program, their friends and families, the rabbi(s), health and mental health professionals, and direct service providers.

II.   Establish the group's identity.

    A.   Agree on terminology, basic halachic perspectives, and focus.

    B.   Bring in outside resource persons when necessary.

III.   Assess needs and catalogue strengths of your congregation.

    A.   Rabbi(s) and lay staff should have the opportunity to develop the knowledge and skills necessary to implement congregational efforts to respond to issues raised by the focus group or task force, including mental illness. Be sure the following areas are covered:

        1.   The nature, severity, and scope of the issues to be addressed, including mental illness, and the effect on individuals, their families, and the community.

        2.   The skills that are necessary to identify behaviors that may indicate a difficulty (including mental illness) for an individual or family.

        3.   The skills that are necessary to become involved in the spiritual needs of those members who must cope with the problems of living, including mental illness for themselves or their families.

    B.   Does a "Caring Community Committee" exist within the congregation?

    C.   Establish a support system for members, including families. This should include people who are returning to the congregation after treatment for an illness, including mental illness, or remaining in the congregation while receiving ongoing treatment.

    D.   Make a survey of available community resources, treatment and educational programs, and self-help organizations.

IV.   Consider what is possible.

    A.   Evaluate what is possible to do within the resources of your congregation and community.

    B.   Set realistic goals within realistic time frames, expecting realistic support and commitment.

    C.   Decide what is doable this year.

V.   Plan and present to your congregation's board a start-up proposal.

    A.   Establish connections and begin building relationships with community agencies, self-help organizations, denominational resource persons, and other congregations.

    B.   Formulate long-term goals and objectives.

        1.   Do you want to offer continuing education for synagogue and community leadership?

        2.   Do you want to establish programs of direct service for persons with mental illness and their families?

        3.   Do you want to establish programs of direct service that serve a variety of needs within the synagogue, including the needs of people with mental illness and their families?

    C.   Establish a time line for action, including a timetable for securing the support of the rabbi(s) and all committees and/or boards.

    D.   Designate spokesperson(s) and assign other tasks, such as

        1.   selecting literature for displays;

        2.   developing a budget;

        3.   identifying possible speakers for synagogue events;

4. locating sample Jewish curriculum materials or those from another denomination; and

5. identifying and interpreting public policy issues.

VI. Continue implementation of long-term strategies.

    A. Give particular attention to recommendations in policy statement(s) of your synagogue's national organization.

    B. Form coalitions with other interested congregations and organizations.

    C. Provide public forums and public service announcements.

    D. Organize education and training events.

    E. Include the program in your synagogue's annual budget.

    F. Provide for ongoing evaluation and reporting to the congregation.

VII. Train volunteers.

    A. Describe the context of the program.

    B. Describe the history and role of the synagogue in the community.

    C. Identify and build on volunteers' strengths and skills.

    D. Discuss the nature of friendship and helping roles, including the limits of advice giving, encouraging responsibility rather than dependence, appropriate degrees of personal involvement, setting limits on relationships, and so forth.

Reaching Out to the Mentally Ill

As you do with other friends, treat someone who has a mental illness as you would want to be treated, with understanding and respect.

When a person with a mental illness	You need to
is withdrawn	initiate relevant conversation
is overstimulated	limit input, do not force discussion
becomes insecure	be accepting
is fearful	stay calm.

When symptoms or medications cause behaviors such as	You need to
disorientation	keep to a known, structured routine
difficulty with conversation	slow down, and perhaps repeat; use simple, short sentences
stress in ordinary situations	create an uncomplicated, predictable environment
trouble remembering	help the person record information
unsound judgment	remain rational and reinforce common sense.

Some symptoms of mental illness are unlike anything you will encounter elsewhere. *You* can't change, but you can refrain from further destroying the person's integrity.

When a person with a mental illness	You need to
is not grounded in reality	listen for kernels of truth, or wait for a better time
believes delusions	avoid arguing
displays little empathy	recognize this as a symptom; try not to respond in kind
has difficulty making contact	make direct contact and keep the initiative
seems totally lacking in self-esteem and motivation	affirm the person's value; treat accomplishments positively.

Fine inner qualities often remain and develop in spite of mental illness. Do not do "for" persons with a mental illness, do "with them," as you do with other persons with other disabilities.

When a person with a mental illness	You can
shows a talent such as music, writing, or art	be open to the person sharing with you
retains an inborn generosity	acknowledge the gifts (which may not always be monetary)
expresses an interest in his or her illness and its consequences	learn together
wants to have a serious discussion	remember, even the most severely ill are rational as much of the time as they are psychotic.

"We are in your congregations, your synagogues. Just think about how many of us there are and how many more of us there are with our families. We want to make friends with you. We want to work with you. We have capacities to help. Give us that chance."

—Gary

"Remember us when you are trying to help us. Give us a chance to use what we have, what our capabilities are. Don't stop us. Let us fail. Let us try again. Let us reach as far as we can. That is the love and compassion we seek from you. If you love us, help us to fly, to soar toward our highest goals."

—David

Addressing the Needs of Families

Mental illness of a loved one affects everyone in the family. Reactions are varied. Some families have trouble dealing with the reality of the illness or feel a tremendous sense of shame and isolation. Some may become overly preoccupied with what has happened. In reaching out to a family in this situation it is important to remember that living with disease can be bewildering and taxing. It is important for everyone to know that the family did not cause the illness; the family is not responsible for it. Self-blame and blame leveled by others are destructive for all concerned.

The following information is designed primarily for the friends, families, and colleagues of the mentally ill and could be made available to them in the form of a brochure or fact sheet.

Families need to plan for the future. Many family members who work together to deal with the often harsh effects of mental illness may discover a wealth of abilities and assets they possess as individuals and as a unit. The family's discovery of these strengths and skills often gives rise to changes that improve the quality of life for everyone in the family (including the ill member). As time goes by the family may find itself the first line of defense for their loved one. They must keep themselves physically and mentally healthy so that they are able to give their best help to their ill family member.

Anyone living and/or working with a person who has a mental illness should:

- Place no blame or guilt
- Look for support
- Seek relief from stress
- Continue outside interests
- Don't try to be "super parent," "super spouse," or "super friend."

The following are some tips to help in coping with a family member who is mentally ill. Families have found these techniques useful. They can be used in developing coping strategies that complement professional treatment.

- Learn all you can about the illness and educate other family members and friends about it.
- Develop/know resources for help and support before a crisis occurs.

95

- Designate someone in the ill person's immediate circle (family member, friend) to be available to help when needed.
- Anticipate vulnerable situations (difficult relationships, job stresses, anniversary and holiday dates), and space them out if possible. If Aunt Tess can't handle the relationship, don't have her to dinner when the ill family member is present.
- Space out stressful events. Remember, what is stressful for your ill family member may not be stressful for you.
- Realize that a person with a mental illness can suffer from memory loss or poor concentration. This is frustrating and frightening. Do not be judgmental.
- Break down tasks into small units so that they do not overwhelm the ill person. Focus on successes.
- Avoid pampering. Set reasonable rules and limits and stick to them. If you find this difficult to do, ask the doctor or counselor for suggestions.
- Avoid expecting that all peculiar behaviors and habits can be corrected.
- Learn about medications—what they are and do, the side effects and residual effects they may have, how they work, and how long they take to work.
- Pay attention to medications (are they being taken, do they seem to be working, etc.).
- Realize that common substances, such as coffee, tea, sugar, alcohol, and over-the-counter medications, may adversely affect the ill person.
- Be sure other doctors know what medications the person is taking.
- Realize that another breakdown may be temporary. The person has recovered before and is likely to do so again.

Programming

A key component of dealing with mental illness in the Jewish community is creating a body of knowledge and awareness within the community itself. Establishing meetings to introduce these concepts at local congregations is one way to increase awareness within the congregational community. The congregation without expertise in this area can partner with outside groups and lend credibility to the project. Support groups are yet another way congregations can reach out to the mentally ill.

Panels

Below are two examples of conferences that were recently held to increase Jewish knowledge about mental illness. These panels were created by and for specific Jewish communities, but their content is applicable throughout the Jewish community as a whole.

Mental Illness and Jewish Families

Presented by Jewish Family Service of Orange County; National Alliance for the Mentally Ill of Orange County; Orange County Board of Rabbis; The Jewish Healing Center of Orange County.

Panelists for "Ask the Doctor": Charles S. Grob, M.D.; Steven Potkin, M.D.; Mark Zetin, M.D.

1. What is mental illness?
2. How are Jews affected differently?
3. What treatments are available?
4. What is the latest research?
5. What family supports are available?
6. Personal experiences of family coping

Opening Doors, Opening Minds, Opening Hearts

The Mental Health Education Project (A Collaborative Program of the Twin Cities Jewish Community)

Breakout Sessions include:

- Healing through Psalms and Songs
- Addiction and Mental Illness: Two Struggles at the Same Time
- Normal vs. Problematical Aging: Depression and Dementia in Older Adults
- Is There a Narrative for My Story? Mental Health and Mental Illness in Biblical Texts
- Caring for the Caregivers

Pair with an Outside Organization

Often, programs on mental illness are not explicitly Jewish. However, by using the physical space of a Jewish organization or congregation, or by lending the name of a congregation for publicity purposes, the clear statement is made that mental illness is an issue important to and for the Jewish community. The following programs are examples of "pairing" to present mental health programming.

- Overcoming the Stigma of Mental Illness: Understanding Manic Depressive (Bipolar) Illness
    Naomi Ruth Cohen Charitable Foundation,
    held at Beth Emeth Free Synagogue; Evanston, Ill.
- Healing the Mind and the Spirit: A Forum for Clergy
    American Foundation for Suicide Prevention
    in partnership with the Cuyahoga Country Community Mental Health Board

Forming a Support Group

Depending on the size of your congregation, you might have the resources to form a support group solely within your own congregation. Many communities, however, have banded together to form support and social groups for members suffering from mental illnesses. The following are some examples of such groups, as well as contact information.

- **Refuah: A Time for Healing:** A Jewish organization dedicated to helping families cope with mental illness. http://www.refuahboston.org
- **ACHRAIYUT:** A Jewish spiritual support group for those experiencing a mental illness. ACHRAIYUT, c/o Temple Israel, 10765 Ladue Road, St. Louis, MO 63141
- **Chaverim Shel Shalom:** A program of the Jewish Family and Children's Service of Boston for people with psychiatric conditions and their friends. C/o Nancy R. Smith, 1340 Centre Street, Newton, MA 02459-2453

Appendix A

Additional Resources

Advocates for the Jewish Mentally Ill
2100 Arch St.
Philadelphia, PA 19103
215-832-0671
A support group for parents of the mentally ill.

Alzheimer's Association
919 North Michigan Ave.
Suite 1100
Chicago, IL 60611-1676
800-272-3900
www.alz.org
Alzheimer's Association has prepared several important brochures that may be helpful to you in dealing with this issue. They include

- "Steps to Getting a Diagnosis: Finding out If It Is Alzheimer's Disease"
- "Living with Early Onset Alzheimer's Disease"
- "Steps to Enhancing Your Home: Modifying the Environment"
- "Steps to Understanding Challenging Behaviors: Responding to the Person with Alzheimer's Disease"
- "Steps to Enhancing Communication: Interacting with Persons with Alzheimer's Disease"
- "Steps to Ensuring Safety: Preventing Wandering and Getting Lost"
- "Steps to Understanding Legal Issues: Planning for the Future"
- "Steps to Assisting with Personal Care: Overcoming Challenges and Adapting to the Needs of Persons with Alzheimer's Disease"
- "Steps to Facing Late-Stage Care: Making End of Life Decisions"
- "Steps to Caring for a Person with Late-Stage Alzheimer's Disease"
- "You Are One of Us: Successful Clergy/Church Connections to Alzheimer's Families"

American Academy of Child and Adolescent Psychiatry
3615 Wisconsin Ave N.W.
Washington, D.C. 20016
202-966-7300
www.aacap.org

American Association of Pastoral Counselors
9504 A Lee Highway
Fairfax, VA 22031-2303
703-385-6967

American Foundation for Suicide Prevention
30195 Chagrin Blvd.
Suite 210 N.
Cleveland, OH 44124
216-464-3471

American Psychiatric Association
1400 K St. N.W.
Washington, D.C. 20005
202-682-6000
202-682-6850 (fax)
www.psych.org

Association of Jewish Family and Children's Agencies
557 Cranberry Rd.
Suite 2
East Brunswick, NJ 08816
800-634-7346

Bay Area Jewish Healing Center
3330 Geary Blvd.
3rd Floor West
San Francisco, CA 94118

Breaking the Silence
A curriculum for elementary through high school students on the reduction of stigma and raising awareness. Available through local NAMI offices.

Chaverim Shel Shalom
A support program of the Jewish Family and Children's Service
1340 Centre St.
Newton, MA 02459-2453

Federation of Families for Children's Mental Health
1101 King St.
Suite 420
Alexandria, VA 22314
703-684-7710

National Alliance for the Mentally Ill (NAMI)
2107 Wilson Blvd.
Suite 300
Arlington, VA 22201
703-524-7600
www.nami.org
Local NAMI chapters often have developed specific resources, such as "Breaking the Silence," a curriculum for religious schools on mental health awareness. This is available from NAMI/Queens-Nassau, 1983 Marcus Ave. C-103, Lake Success, N.Y. 11042.

National Alliance for Research on Schizophrenia and Depression
60 Cutter Mill Rd.
Suite 404
Great Neck, NY 11021
516-829-0091
www.mhsource.com/narsad

National Center for Jewish Healing
850 Seventh Ave.
Suite 1201
New York, NY 10019
212-399-2320

National Depressive and Manic Depressive Association
730 N. Franklin
Suite 501
Chicago, IL 60610
312-642-0049
www.ndmda.org

National Institute for Mental Health
Division of Communications
5600 Fishers Lane
Rockville, MD 20857
301-443-3783
www.nimh.nih.gov

National Mental Health Association
2001 North Beauregard St.
12th Floor
Alexandria, VA 22311
703-684-7722
www.nmha.org

Obsessive Compulsive Disorder Foundation
P.O. Box 9573
New Haven, CT 06066
203-772-0565

Pathways to Promise
5400 Arsenal St.
St. Louis, MO 63139-1484
314-644-8834 (fax)
www.pathways2promise.org
An interfaith clearinghouse and resource center on mental health issues

REFUAH
15 Hemlock Terrace
Randolph, MA 02368
781-961-2815
nblrefuah@aol.com
Jewish resource center for families and individuals dealing with mental health issues

Schizophrenia and Bipolar Illness in the Jewish Community
A Johns Hopkins University Study of Ashkenazi Jews
Dr. Ann E. Pulver, Principal Investigator
Johns Hopkins University
School of Medicine
Department of Psychiatry
Baltimore, MD 21231
1-888-289-4095
aepulver@welchlink.welch.jhu.edu

Union of American Hebrew Congregations
Department of Jewish Family Concerns
633 3rd Ave.
7th Floor
New York, NY 10017
212-650-4294
deptjewfamcon@uahc.org

Appendix B

Responsa and Resolutions
Regarding Mental Illness

Both the Central Conference of American Rabbis and the Union of American Hebrew Congregations have addressed the issue of mental illness, both in responsa and in resolutions. This section includes many of the Reform responsa related to the issue of mental illness, as well as the two most recent CCAR and UAHC resolutions.

Conversion of a Person Suffering from Mental Illness

CCAR Responsa 5758.7

She'elah

A woman in my congregation, married to a Jewish man, has been coming to me to study for conversion to Judaism. Her own religious background is quite mixed, and she feels no particular attachment to any other faith. She has some knowledge of Judaism, and has been reading and studying with me for about six months. I believe she is sincere about wanting to convert to Judaism, although some of the motivation undoubtedly comes from her in-laws. In my opinion, however, she is not mentally stable.

The first thing she told me when we met was that she was a borderline personality who had been sexually abused by both of her parents. In the fairly brief time I have known her she has been on the verge of divorce twice, stated that her husband was abusing her, changed therapists, and asked if she could bring her dog into the sanctuary with her for emotional solace in a new environment. She often makes very dramatic statements, only to back away from them later. From everything I have been able to learn, she is quite clearly a borderline personality, a well-recognized diagnosis of significant mental illness. She is not, however, insane or incapable of making decisions for herself.

May I reject her as a candidate for conversion on grounds of her mental illness?

Teshuvah

1. Mental Competence and Mental Illness. The possession of mental competence (*da'at* or *de'ah*) is one of the principal requirements for conversion to Judaism. This is because conversion is understood as the acceptance by a Gentile of the mitzvot, the obligations of Jewish life.[1]

---

[1] On the process of *kabalat hamitzvot* by a proselyte, see BT *Yevamot* 47a–b; *Yad, Isurey Bi'ah* 14:1–5; *SA* YD 268:2–3. Conversion is commonly portrayed in the sources as the ritual and spiritual equivalent of the acceptance of the Torah by our ancestors at Sinai; see BT *Keritot* 9a and *Yad, Isurey Bi'ah* 13:1–5, along with BT *Yevamot* 46a, and Rashi, *s.v. be'avoteinu shemalu.*

One who is mentally incompetent is not judged legally accountable for his or her actions;[2] therefore, a Jew who lacks *da'at* is exempt from the duty to perform the mitzvot.[3] Accordingly, the Jew-by-choice who seeks to enter the community of mitzvot must be able to understand the nature of the duties he or she is accepting and to be held responsible for them. As our Committee has written in a similar case: "Conversion to Judaism is a major religious step which cannot be taken lightly; this act has legal [halachic] implications . . . [since] a complete understanding of Judaism is necessary for a sincere and complete conversion, such prospective converts must be of sound mind and mentally competent. We cannot accept individuals who do not meet these prerequisites."[4]

For these reasons, it is clear that we are entitled and even required to reject a candidate for conversion should we find that he or she does not possess the necessary mental competence. The question we face here is whether this prospective proselyte fits that concept. Does she, on account of her emotional disturbance, lack the "sound mind" necessary to make the responsible choice to enter the covenant of Israel?

To ask this question is to ask whether, in the terms of our tradition, this woman exhibits the characteristics of the *shoteh/ah,* the "insane" person, who by definition does not possess *da'at* and is thereby exempted from any and all responsibility to uphold the mitzvot.[5] The talmudic sources identify the *shoteh* as one who wanders alone at night, who sleeps in the cemetery, who rips his or her clothing, or who loses everything that is given to him or her.[6] The halakhic consensus holds that a person need not exhibit all of these behaviors to be defined as a *shoteh;* one of them alone is sufficient, provided that the action is performed regularly and in such a way that it offers evidence of insanity.[7] There is considerable disagreement in the literature as to whether insanity *(shetut)* is to be identified by these actions in particular or whether they are to be seen as examples of a more general condition. Some authorities regard the list in talmudic sources as exhaustive: "We have nothing to rely upon except the words of our Sages."[8] Maimonides, on the other hand, takes the opposite view. The *shoteh* of whom we speak is not only the one "who walks about naked, breaking things and throwing stones," but rather "one who has lost his mind and whose mind is consistently disturbed with respect to any matter, even though he speaks rationally on all other matters."[9]

---

[2]*M. Bava Kama* 8:4; *Yad, Chovel Umazik* 4:20; *SA* CM 424:8.

[3]BT *Chagigah* 2b and Rashi, 2a, *s.v. chutz:* the deaf-mute *(cheresh),* the insane person *(shoteh),* and the minor *(katan)* are exempt from the obligation to perform the mitzvot on the ground that "they do not possess *de'ah.*" See also *M. Rosh Hashanah* 3:8: these same individuals cannot sound the shofar on behalf of others because they themselves are not "obligated with respect to this act." See *Yad,* Edut 9:9: the *shoteh* is not qualified to serve as a witness because "he is not subject to the mitzvot"; and *Yad,* Chametz Umatzah 6:4 (based upon BT *Rosh Hashanah* 28a): one who performs a mitzvah during a moment of insanity has not fulfilled his obligation, for at that moment he was "exempt from all the mitzvot."

[4]*American Reform Responsa (ARR),* no. 67. The *she'elah* there dealt with a prospective convert described as "mentally unbalanced (paranoid)."

[5]See *M. Arakhin* 1:1 and the sources cited in note 3.

[6]*Tosefta Terumot* 1:3; BT *Chagigah* 3b–4a; PT *Terumot* 1:1 (40b) and parallels.

[7]*Hil. HaRosh, Chulin* 1:4, following the view of R. Yochanan and the *setam talmud* in BT *Chagigah* 3b–4a; *SA Yore De'ah* 1:5; R. Shelomo Luria, *Yam Shel Shelomo, Chulin* 1:4.

[8]R. Yosef Kolon (fifteenth-century Italy), *Resp. Maharik Hachadashot,* no. 20, quotes R. Avigdor Hakohen (thirteenth-century Germany) in a *teshuvah* to R. Meir of Rothenburg: "One who is not judged a *shoteh* by the actions mentioned in the first chapter of *Chagigah* [3b] must be declared mentally competent in all respects." R. Yitzchak b. Sheshet, it would seem, also reads the talmudic list as exhaustive; *Resp. Rivash,* nos. 20 and 468. And R. Yosef Karo, in *SA* YD 1:5, defines the *shoteh* as one who exhibits the behaviors mentioned in the Talmud. See, however, note 9.

[9]*Yad,* Edut 9:9–10. See R. Yosef Karo's discussion in *Beit Yosef,* EHE 121. Karo adopts Maimonides's definition of the *shoteh* in *SA* CM 35:8, thereby creating a difficulty against his ruling in YD 1:5.

This position surely strikes us as the more reasonable one, since it is difficult to imagine a plausible definition of insanity that restricts itself to but three or four specific actions out of a host of others that are clearly symptomatic of serious mental disturbance. As noted above, even a person who exhibits those behaviors is not judged insane by talmudic standards unless they are performed in a manner that indicates insanity (*derekh shetut*),[10] thus, "insanity" is better understood as a *manner* of behavior, a state of mental disturbance that can express itself in any number of ways, rather than as a catalogue of several specific acts.[11] Although contemporary Orthodox halakhists tend not to decide between the two sides of this legal dispute,[12] they are capable of recognizing that judgments in this area are necessarily complex. As one puts it: "It is impossible to define with precision just who is called a '*shoteh*' in our time, or more properly, at which stage (of an illness) a person is defined as 'insane' and exempt from the *mitzvot*.... On account of the wide variety of psychiatric ailments along with the many specific forms of behavior, which can change from time to time due to natural causes or as a result of treatment, we are required to judge each case separately, in accordance with the opinion of experts and the judgment of the rabbinic authority or *beit din*."[13] For our part, we hold that the definition of mental illness is to be made by observation and is a matter of medicine and psychology, properly determined by the accepted procedures of those disciplines. As we have written, "given our positive attitude as liberal Jews toward modernity in general, it is surely appropriate to rely upon the findings of modern science, rather than upon tenuous analogies from traditional sources, in order to render what we must consider to be scientific judgments."[14] We think that this position accurately reflects the view of Maimonides, applied in the context of the scientific and cultural realities of our time.

None of this, of course, renders the answer to this *she'elah* a simple one. Even if we accept this woman's testimony that she suffers from an emotional disorder, we may not be in a position to declare that she does not possess the requisite mental competence we demand of a person who chooses Judaism. To be sure, borderline personality disorder (BPD) is a serious condition, and those afflicted with it "present a variety of neurotic symptoms and character defects."[15] They may, we are told, fail to establish their own identities. They may be emotionally unbalanced and impulsive, display multiple phobias, obsessive thoughts and behaviors, and paranoid traits. They may be constantly angry and frequently depressed, sexually promiscuous,

---

[10]BT *Chagigah* 3b.

[11]We might echo in this regard the rhetorical question posed by R. Ya'akov Weil (fifteenth-century Germany, *Responsa*, no. 52): "Consider the one who does *not* rend his garments, does *not* sleep in the cemetery and does *not* wander alone at night and yet acts in an insane manner in all other respects. Is he not to be judged insane?" Other *poskim* suggest that the "symptoms" mentioned in BT *Chagigah* do not *define* insanity but are rather standards by which to measure insanity in its most obvious and extreme manifestation. Thus, R. Yosef Kolon (see note 8), who does not decide the *machloket* between Maimonides and the opposing view, writes that "if one agrees that the 'signs' of insanity mentioned in *Chagigah* are not exhaustive and that the Sages were simply giving examples ... [this means that] one should examine to see whether a person has reached an extreme level of *shetut* such as evidenced by these behaviors." This position is accepted explicitly by R. Yechezkel Landau (eighteenth-century Prague), in a responsum included in the book *Or Hayashar* (ch. 30), an eighteenth-century work containing rabbinical responsa over the validity of a *get* issued by a husband who may or may not have been "insane."

[12]See R. A. S. Avraham, *Nishmat Avraham* 3:181, who recites the *machloket* but does not attempt to resolve it directly.

[13]*Ibid.*, 181–82.

[14]Responsum no. 5757.2.

[15]A. M. Freedman, M.D., Harold I. Kaplan, M.D., and P. J. Sadock, M.D., eds., *Comprehensive Textbook of Psychiatry*, 2d ed. (Baltimore: Williams and Wilkins Co., 1975), 550. The medical information in this paragraph is taken from that source and from Benjamin B. Wolman, editor-in-chief, *The Encyclopedia of Psychiatry, Psychology, and Psychoanalysis* (New York: Henry Holt, 1996), 83.

and have a pronounced tendency toward drug and alcohol abuse. They are unable to develop lasting relationships in marriage and career. They are quite difficult as patients, often attempting to manipulate their therapists in order to gain needed gratification. Many of them threaten suicide, and some of them are indeed suicidal. All of this may be true of BPD individuals in general and of this woman in particular, yet this is still not enough to say that she, the individual whose case we are addressing here, is a *shotah*, lacking the *da'at* or capacity to make rational decisions and judgments about herself and her life. We should not forget that a medical term such as "borderline personality disorder" is simply a name given to a particular constellation of "neurotic symptoms and character defects." It is a category utilized by the mental health professions as a means of classifying data and determining courses of treatment. It is a description of a general phenomenon which in and of itself does not tell us that *this* woman is "insane." Put another way, while this woman may be "mentally ill," we do not know by that token that she is mentally *incompetent*. The diagnosis, assuming it is an accurate one, cannot serve as a substitute for a careful examination of her character, her strengths and weaknesses, her "defects," and her resiliency in overcoming or compensating for them.

This is merely another way of saying that "general principles do not decide concrete cases;"[16] or, as Maimonides remarks in his discussion of mental competence, "Since it is impossible to define '*da'at*' with full precision in writing, the matter must be decided by the judge in the particular instance."[17] To translate this insight into the terms of the present *she'elah*, we cannot say this individual is unfit for conversion based upon a diagnosis that she suffers from a general syndrome known as "borderline personality disorder." Such a determination can be based only upon a finding that *this* person, this individual human being, lacks the mental competence we think necessary to make an informed and rational choice for Judaism.

2. Proper and Improper Motivations for Conversion. Yet the definition of "insanity" is not the only issue here. Our case turns as well upon the question of proper motivations for conversion to Judaism, which the Talmud discusses in two places. In the first, which describes what we must call the ideal state, the prospective proselyte is warned of all the hardships and dangers that await him should he become a Jew; if he says, "would that I merit to participate in their suffering!," he is accepted forthwith.[18] The second text speaks not of the pure religious motivations of the ideal candidate but of those that inspire other sorts of individuals. It tells us that, in principle *(lekhatchilah),* we should not accept proselytes who wish to convert in order to marry a Jew, or who seek to join us out of a desire to share in our good fortune, or who come to Judaism in response to fear or threats, real or imagined, although should such persons undergo a valid process of conversion they are nonetheless considered proselytes.[19] The medieval commentators raised a difficulty against this "in principle" standard, noting several examples of talmudic sages who accepted as proselytes individuals who came before them with evidently improper motives. They resolved the difficulty by suggesting that in those cases the sages were confident that the proselytes who came originally out of ulterior motivations would ultimately accept the Torah "for the sake of Heaven."[20] And on the basis of that resolu-

---

[16] The quotation is taken from the famous dissent of U.S. Supreme Court Justice Oliver Wendell Holmes, Jr. in *Lochner v. New York,* 198 U.S. 45, 74 (1905). Holmes continued that "the decision will depend on a judgment or intuition more subtle than any articulate major premise." This notion is a key to the understanding of legal reasoning, no less applicable to the halakhic tradition than to any other system of law.

[17] *Yad, Edut* 9:10.

[18] BT *Yevamot* 47a and Rashi, *s.v. ve'eini kedai; Yad, Isurey Bi'ah* 14:1; *SA* YD 268:2.

[19] BT *Yevamot* 24b, including the mishnah (M. *Yevamot* 2:8); *Yad, Isurey Bi'ah* 13:14–17; *SA* YD 268:12.

[20] *Tosafot, Yevamot* 24b, *s.v. lo.* The exceptional cases are those involving Hillel (BT *Shabbat* 31a) and R. Chiya (BT *Menachot* 44a).

tion, later authorities declare: "We learn from this that (with respect to conversion) the entire matter is left to the judgment of the *beit din.*"[21]

This, as far as we are concerned, is a chief guiding principle in our thinking about conversion. It is for the *beit din,* the religious tribunal under the supervision of the presiding rabbi, to determine in each and every case whether the person who comes before us for conversion does so for reasons that are appropriate. Occasionally, Orthodox authorities will rely upon this discretionary power in order to accept proselytes who wish to become Jews for reasons that fall far short of the ideal standard of pure religious conviction.[22] Yet whether for leniency or stringency, the decision is in any event for the authorities to make. On this point we are in full agreement with Orthodox halakhic thinking. Conversion, for us no less than for other Jews, is not a decision left to the heart and mind of the proselyte but is a formal and public matter. One who seeks to convert seeks to join our community as a full and participating "citizen" thereof. It is accordingly for the Jewish community, acting through its acknowledged rabbinical representatives, to determine in each and every case whether an individual who wishes to convert is in fact ready to do so, for reasons that we find persuasive and compelling.

Let us turn this insight to the present case. If the rabbi under whose guidance this woman is studying believes that she is ready for conversion, that she fully understands the fateful nature of this step and is preparing to undertake it out of motivations that strike him as credible and appropriate, then he is entitled (and perhaps even obligated)[23] to accept her as a Jew-by-choice. On the other hand, should the rabbi find that there is significant doubt as to this woman's mental and emotional readiness to make a thoughtful, careful, and responsible decision to convert to Judaism, he is entitled (and perhaps required) to reject her candidacy. The burden of proof, that is to say, is upon the candidate to demonstrate her readiness and not upon the rabbi to demonstrate the opposite. His decision need not be based upon preponderant evidence that she is "insane" and lacking in *da'at.* He may even find, as he tells us in his *she'elah,* that she is "sincere" in her desire to convert. Yet so long as he is not convinced that she is ready to take this step, so long as he has good reason to believe that her desire to convert is reflective of an emotional pathology rather than what can be defined as a reasonable and responsible choice, he is definitely under no obligation to accept her.

Conclusion. The rabbi may indeed reject this woman as a candidate for conversion, although not simply on the grounds of mental illness. A finding that she is "mentally ill" or even that she displays a condition as serious as borderline personality disorder does not necessarily in and of itself prove that she is lacking in *da'at,* the ability to make responsible and appropriate choices. The term "mental illness" is a broad descriptive category and not a diagnosis of the fitness of the individual person; we should beware of taking any step that suggests that those who suffer from "mental illness" are to be labelled as "insane." He may reject her rather on the grounds that *this* decision, in his carefully considered opinion, is motivated by factors that call its rationality and appropriateness into serious question. In any event, "the entire matter is left to the discretion of the *beit din.*"

---

[21] *Beit Yosef,* YD 268; *Siftey Kohen,* YD 268, no. 23.

[22] Among the examples: R. Shelomo Kluger, *Resp. Tuv ta'am veda'at,* no. 230; R. David Zvi Hoffmann, *Resp. Melamed leho'il* 2:83, 85; R. Benzion Ouziel, *Resp. Mishpetey ouziel,* YD, no. 14, and EHE, no. 18.

[23] See BT *Yevamot* 47b: once a candidate has demonstrated his full and informed acceptance of the mitzvot, "he is circumcised immediately." Why, asks the Gemara, do we do this *immediately?* Because "we do not delay the performance of a mitzvah."

89. Funeral Service for a Suicide

American Reform Responsa (Vol. LXIX, 1959, pp. 120–23)

QUESTION: A member of our congregation committed suicide and the question arose as to the funeral service. Should there be a eulogy, and should the services be simplified and the mourning ritual diminished?

ANSWER: The question of suicides and the funeral rituals that are permitted or forbidden with regard to them has long occupied the attention of Jewish legal authorities. Our Conference itself had an elaborate discussion on it in the year 1923. This discussion ended with a brief statement by the late Dr. Jacob Z. Lauterbach, chairman of our Responsa Committee. The statement consisted of one short paragraph in which Dr. Lauterbach stated the general tendency of the law to seek for reasons to keep from declaring a man to be a suicide. This question has come up very often since 1923, and occasionally involves painful discussions with the family of the deceased. Therefore, the subject, so highly complex, should now be clarified and some conclusion arrived at. The following responsum, therefore, is an attempt at some general line of procedure with regard to this situation.

Surprisingly enough, there is no clear law against suicide in the Bible or the Talmud. Perhaps suicide was so rare that there was no need for such a law. The Bible mentions only two suicides in the entire long span of history that it covers: King Saul on Mount Gilboa (1 Samuel 31:4) and David's counselor, Ahitophel (2 Samuel 17:23). Nor does the Talmud find it necessary to speak of the sin of suicide. Some of the earlier scholars base the objection to this crime upon the verse used by God to Noah when he and his family left the Ark: "Surely your blood of your lives will I require" (Genesis 9:5). But neither Maimonides nor Aaron Halevi in the *Chinuch* count this as one of the negative commandments.

The first clear-cut statement about the crime of suicide is in the post-Talmudic booklet *S'machot,* at the beginning of chapter 2. There it is stated that those who commit suicide are to receive no burial rites. The phraseology used there is important, since from this source it

has found its way into all important later discussions. "He who destroys himself consciously *(lada-at)*, we do not engage ourselves with his funeral in any way. We do not tear the garments, and we do not bare the shoulder in mourning, and we do not say eulogies for him;
but we do stand in the mourner's row and recite the blessing of the mourners because the
latter is for the honor of the living." Then follows a definition of the crime of suicide as
follows: If a man is found hanged or fallen from a tree or a wall he is not to be deemed a
suicide unless he says, "I am going to do so," and they see him climb up, etc. Then it is stated that a child who commits suicide is not to be counted as a suicide, clearly because he is
not to be judged as acting with a clear mind *(lada-at)*, which must be presupposed before
the crime is to be considered a crime. Then follows the law that those convicted and executed by the Jewish courts should not be mourned for in any way lest the mourning imply
that the Sanhedrin had made an unjust judgment.

From this statement in *S'machot* the law spread to all the codes and frequently appears in
the Responsa literature. In this original source it is evident that only a person who commits suicide with a clear mind and with an announced intention beforehand is to be treated as a suicide. A mere presumption of suicide is not sufficient.

This desire to be cautious with the accusation of suicide had many motives, of course.
One was that the law itself spoke of circumstances under which one should willingly accept
death, when threatened with the compulsion to violate any of the three sins of idolatry,
immorality, and murder (B. *Sanhedrin* 74a). This type of suicide, often carried out in wholesale fashion in the Middle Ages as well as in earlier times, was honored as noble martyrdom.
Therefore, it was clear that not all surrender of life could be deemed blameworthy by the
law. At times it was even noble. Thus, the Talmud speaks in praise of the mass suicide by
drowning of young boys and girls being taken captive for a shameful life in Rome (B. *Gittin*
57b). Besides martyrdom, the law also considered personal stresses. Thus, the tradition never
seems to have blamed King Saul for his suicide. In fact, his case became a frequently cited
case in the following way: King Saul was afraid that the Philistines would subject him to
torture, and he saw himself as dying anyhow, and therefore, while the sin is still a sin, it is a
forgivable one.

With Saul as a pardonable prototype for most suicides under stress, the Rabbis, in many
a specific case that came before them, sought and found reasons why a person who took
his own life should not be stigmatized legally as a suicide. They generally said that whoever is under stress as Saul was *(anus keSha ul)*, is not to be considered a suicide legally, even
if he takes his own life. A number of cases will indicate their considerate mood in this
regard.

Jacob Weil, a German rabbi of the thirteenth–fourteenth century, in his Responsa (no.
114) speaks of the case of a Jewish criminal who was executed by the German courts.
Should not such a criminal be deemed equivalent to a suicide (since he willfully risked his
life) and therefore not have a regular burial and be mourned for? He gives a number of reasons why this man should be mourned for with full mourning ritual. First, he was tortured,
and pain is considered a purification of sin. Then, we assume, he made confession of his sins,
and that, too, brought him atonement. So Mordecai Benet, Rabbi of Nicholsburg, in the
early nineteenth century (*Parashat Mordechai,* Yoreh De-a 25), discusses a criminal who was
found in his cell, having committed suicide. He says that such an act is to be called suicide
only if it is done with full and clear awareness *(lada-at)*. This man certainly was in terror of
being executed, or of being imprisoned for life in the dungeons of the city of Bruenn,
which is worse than death; therefore he is to be considered as having acted under unbear-

able stress, as King Saul was. In general, he said that a man is not wholly responsible for what he does in his grief.

Solomon Kluger of Brody (middle of the nineteenth century, *Ha-elef Lecha Shelomo,* Yoreh De-a 301) speaks of a man heavily in debt who attempted suicide, failed, and some days afterwards died. First, there was a question of whether he really died because of the wound he inflicted on himself; secondly, he was under great stress; and Kluger concludes that whoever is under stress, as Saul was, is not to be considered a suicide. Also based upon the original source in the baraita *S'machot,* chapter 2, all children who for some reason or other commit suicide are not to be treated as legal suicides because they certainly cannot be assumed to act *lada-at,* with full knowledge.

A summary of the thoughtful, sympathetic attitude of the law to such unfortunates is summed up in the latest code, *Aruch Hashulchan,* Yoreh De-a 345 (Yechiel Epstein). He says, in general summary: "We seek all sorts of reasons possible to explain away the man's action, either his fear, or his pain, or temporary insanity, in order not to declare the man a suicide." Whatever the secular coroner or medical examiner would declare, the concern of Judaism, which deals with a man's religious rights, depends upon what Jewish traditional law says and feels. It would amount to this: Only a man who commits suicide calmly and with clear resolve is to be considered a suicide. In fact, some of the scholars say that he has first to announce his intention and then to fulfill it at once. If he announces such intention and is found dead much later, or if he is found dead under suspicious circumstances but did not declare such an intention, he is not to be treated as a suicide.

Since the definition for legal suicide was so strict, there were many cases of presumed suicides that were not definitely so stigmatized. Therefore, the scholars could allow themselves to permit full funeral rights for many whom—out of kindness—they declared as not being legal suicides. They were frequently uncertain as to how much ritual should be permitted. The original source in *S'machot* says that there must be no mourning at all—no tearing of garments, no eulogies, no mourning rituals after the burial. In fact, it begins by saying, "We do not deal with them at all" *("Ein mitasekin bahem"),* which would imply that we do nothing even about burial. But, inasmuch as they were loath to declare anybody a suicide, they proceeded, as it were, to nibble away at the wholesale prohibitions just described.

The strictest of all codifiers is Maimonides *(Hilchot Evel),* who says that there should be no mourning rites, etc., but only the blessing for the mourners. The Ramban, in *Toledot Ha-adam,* says that there should be tearing of the garments. The next step is taken by Solomon ben Adret, the great legal authority of Barcelona (thirteenth century) in his Responsum no. 763. He says that certainly we are in duty bound to provide shrouds and burial. A later authority, Moses Sofer, in his Responsa, Yoreh De-a 326, says that we certainly do say *Kaddish,* and he would permit any respectable family to go through all the mourning ritual, lest the family have to bear innocently eternal disgrace if they do not exercise mourning conspicuously.

The one part of the mourning ritual about which there is almost no permission is the custom of giving a eulogy of the dead. Thus, Jacob Castro, in his notes to the *Shulchan Aruch,* while saying in general that public mourning is forbidden but private mourning is permitted, adds emphatically that we do not give a eulogy and certainly do not have a professional eulogist. Why they were increasingly lenient about mourning rituals but were firm against eulogy is easily understood. Although the man who committed suicide may be pardoned, he should not be praised as an example. In the words of Rabbi Akiva, in the original source in *S'machot:* "We should neither praise nor defame him." In other words, he should be quietly forgiven. Nevertheless, there are one or two opinions that would permit even a eulogy. One is Ezekiel Katzenellenbogen, Rabbi of Altona, of the early eighteenth century (*Keneset Yechezkel,* no. 37), who says that whenever there is any sort of reason, we eulogize him. And the other is the statement in the Talmud specifically about Saul, the prototype, that the children of Israel were punished because they failed to eulogize Saul adequately (B. *Y'vamot* 78b). But, in general, the mood was as summarized by the *Pitchei Teshuva,* Abraham Zevi Eisenstadt, who said: "We mourn but we do not eulogize."

The long and complicated succession of discussions in the law on the matter of suicide amounts, then, to this: An increasing reluctance to stigmatize a man as a suicide, and therefore, an increasing willingness to grant more and more rights of burial and mourning. The only hesitation is with regard to eulogy. It would therefore seem to be in accord with the mood of tradition if we conducted full services and omitted the eulogy, provided this omission does not cause too much grief to the family. If the family is deeply desirous of some address to be given in the funeral service, then the address should be as little as possible in the form of a eulogy of the departed and more in the form of consoling of the survivors. For the general principle is frequently repeated in discussing this law: "That which is for the honor of the living shall be done."

—Solomon B. Freehof

Disabled Persons*

CCAR Responsa 5752.5

She'elah

What are the obligations of the community, and specifically of congregations, toward physically and mentally disabled persons? (CCAR Committee on Justice and Peace)

Teshuvah

Jewish tradition speaks repeatedly of the role that elderly, deaf, blind, and mentally and physically handicapped persons play in the ritual and ceremonial realm, but there is little discussion of the community's obligation toward such persons. What follows is a brief overview of the relevant attitudes found in the biblical and rabbinic sources, and the Reform perspectives we might bring to them.

1. Blind Persons

We are obligated to treat a blind person *(ivver)* with special consideration. For example, the Torah prohibits putting a stumbling block before the blind and warns, "Cursed be the one who causes the blind to wander out of the way."[1]

However, tradition saw the blind as lacking certain legal and ritual capacities[2] and a talmudic passage contains different opinions about issues affecting the sightless. What is

---

*One might well consult *Who Makes People Different,* Carl Astor, United Synagogue of America: New York, 1985, for an even more in-depth analysis of this topic.

[1] Leviticus 19:14 and Deuteronomy 27:18.

[2] For example, BT *Gittin* 2:5, 22b prohibits a blind person from delivering a *get* (the religious divorce document). M. *T'rumot* 1:6 does not allow a blind person to separate *terumah* (a special donation to priests and sanctuary). M. *M'gillah* 3:6 and BT *M'gillah* 24a teach that a person blind from birth may not recite the *Sh'ma* and its blessings for the congregation since s/he would not have experienced the light mentioned in the morning prayer, but this is overruled by the Gemara.

remarkable about it is that, at its end, a blind Torah scholar's reaction to the discussion becomes "the last word" on the matter:

> R. Joseph [who was blind] stated: Formerly I used to say: "If someone would tell me that the halachah is in accordance with R. Judah, who declared that a blind person is exempt from the commandments, I would make a feast for our Rabbis, because though I am not obligated I still perform commandments." But I have heard the statement of R. Hanina, who said that greater is the reward of those who are commanded to do [mitzvot] than of those who without being commanded [do them of their own free will]. If someone would tell me that the halachah is [after all] not in accordance with R. Judah, I would make a feast for our Rabbis, because if I am enjoined to perform commandments the reward will be greater for me.[3]

In general, the halachah goes with R. Hanina and obligates the blind to observe all the commandments, though there were numerous discussions about it.[4] Thus, while the *Shulchan Aruch* rules that the blind may not say the blessing over the *havdalah* candles, other authorities permit them to recite all the benedictions for the ceremony.[5] Further, the blind are obligated to wear *tzitzit,* even though the wording of Numbers 15:39 would seem to demand eyesight for the fulfillment of this mitzvah.[6] We also learn that two blind rabbis recited the Pesach Haggadah for themselves as well as others.[7]

2. Deaf Persons

The deaf person *(cheresh)* is dealt with in the Mishnah:

> We have learnt: "Wherever the Sages speak of *cheresh,* [it means] one who can neither hear nor speak." This [would imply] that he who can speak but not hear, or hear but not speak is obligated [to do all mitzvot]. We have [thus] learnt what our Rabbis taught: One who can speak but not hear is termed *cheresh:* one who can hear but not speak is termed *illeim* [mute]; both are deemed sensible in all that relates to them.

This passage is contradictory in that it offers two definitions of the word *cheresh,* one who is a deaf-mute and one who is simply deaf.

> Said Ravina, and according to others, Rava: [Our mishnah] is defective and should read thus: All are bound to appear [at the Temple] and to rejoice (Deuteronomy 16:14), except a *cheresh* that can speak but not hear, [or] hear but not speak, who is

---

[3]BT *Bava Kama* 86b.

[4]*Tosafot* (medieval talmudic comments, a genre begun by Rashi's descendants) on BT *Bava Kama* 87a. Others argue that even if the law does not require the blind to observe the commandments, their own desire to observe them becomes, in effect, an obligation to do so. See *Chiddushey HaRashba,* BT *Bava Kama* 87a. However, Rambam disqualifies blind persons from serving as witnesses (*Yad, Hilkhot Edut,* 9:12; Sh.A., HM 35:12; *Resp. Tashbetz,* v. 3, #6. See also R. Asher b.Yechiel, *Resp. Ha-Rosh* 4:21, R. Shelomo Luria, *Yam Shel Shelomo, Bava Kama* 8:20, Meirie to BT *Bava Kama* 87a and Mishnah Berurah to Sh.A., OH 53, 41.

[5]The reason for denying them the privilege arises from the argument that, in order to say a blessing over light, one must be able to enjoy its benefits.

[6]Numbers Rabbah, Sh'lach Lecha 17:5, BT *M'nachot* 43a–b, and Sh.A., OH 17:1.

[7]R. Sheshet and the above-cited R. Joseph; BT *P'sachim* 116b.

exempt from appearing [at the Temple]; but though he is exempt from appearing, he is obligated to rejoice. One, however, that can neither hear nor speak (as well as a *shoteh* [simpleton]) and a minor are exempt from rejoicing, since they are exempt from all the precepts stated in the Torah.[8]

In our day, R. Eliezer Waldenberg holds that anyone who can hear anything at all, including by use of a hearing aid, and anyone who can speak are considered *pikei'ach* (as if without disability) and therefore obligated regarding all mitzvot, except those that require hearing. They are married *d'oraita* (based on Torah law directly) and require biblically ordained divorce.[9] Under this very limited definition of *cheresh,* most people with hearing and speaking disabilities will be considered as having no handicap.

Similarly, R. David Bleich maintains that the ability to speak, no matter how acquired and even if the speech acquired is imperfect, is sufficient to establish full competence in all areas of halachah.[10] However, he notes that the status of a normal person who subsequently becomes a deaf-mute is the subject of controversy among halachic authorities. Some consider them to be like congenital deaf-mutes, while others hold that such persons are not to be regarded as legally incompetent.[11]

The development of schools for the deaf was one of the greatest factors in liberalizing halachic thinking regarding deaf and mute persons. R. Isaac Herzog, chief rabbi of Israel until 1959, ruled that "those [rabbis] who remain in the ivory tower and say the schools [for the deaf] are not good enough do not realize the techniques that have been developed in the schools." He goes on to describe the techniques used in the schools and suggests that once they are known, one's point of view must change: "You have got to do so and then remove all limitations that still exist surrounding the technically deaf-mute."[12]

3. Otherwise Physically Disabled Persons

Little systematic consideration is found in rabbinic sources regarding their needs. Such handicapped persons are permitted to recite the *m'gillah* while standing or sitting. We find a discussion about prostheses worn on Shabbat, and such exceptional circumstances as a woman's ability to perform *chalitzah* (the removal of a shoe from her brother-in-law who refuses to marry her)[13] when her hand was amputated. The Sages generally attempted to include handicapped or disfigured individuals in public ceremonies, except when their participation would cause people to gawk at them rather than concentrate on worship.[14]

---

[8]BT *Chagigah* 2a; the cited passage is from M. *T'rumot* 1:2.

[9]Resp. Tzitz Eliezer, 15, # 46, p. 120 ff.

[10]"Survey of Recent Halakhic Periodical Literature: Status of the Deaf-Mute in Jewish Law," *Tradition* 16, no. 5 (fall 1977): 80.

[11]Ibid. Note that Bach, Sh. A., YD 1; Shakh, Sh. A., YD 1:22; and Divrei Chaim, II, EH, # 72, take the former position, and Rambam and Bertinoro (in their commentaries on M. *T'rumot* 1:2) adopt the latter.

[12]Jerome D. Schein and Lester J. Walman, eds. *The Deaf Jew in the Modern World* (New York, 1986), 17.

[13]BT *Shabbat* 65b and *Y'vamot* 105a. The latter tractate is devoted to this biblically ordained ceremony, which obtained when a married man died before he could sire a child. His brother was then obligated to marry the widow in order to "build up a name" for his deceased brother. In modern Israel, the brother is no longer permitted to marry his sister-in-law, but the ceremony of *chalitzah* is still necessary in order to release her so that she can marry again.

[14]See e.g., the question of whether a priest whose hands are discolored may lift them in blessing the congregation; BT *M'gillah* 24b.

4. Mentally Disabled Persons

The word *shoteh* ("simpleton," "imbecile," or "idiot") has generally been taken to refer to a mentally disabled individual. However, close examination of the use of the word in the Mishnah and Talmud reveals that there are two basic kinds of *shotim:* (1) the mentally ill and the retarded (little distinction is made between the two), and (2) the morally deficient who do not act in accordance with the communal ethos, though having the intelligence to do so.

Tradition identified particular types of behavior as falling in category (1) of the definition: One that goes out alone at night, spends the night in a cemetery, tears his garments, or always loses things.[15] Clearly, these activities were meant to characterize the mentally ill rather than the retarded.

In our day, R. Moshe Feinstein differentiated between a *peti* (the mentally retarded whom the community must provide with an education once s/he has reached the understanding of a six-year-old) and the *shoteh*. He urged the welcoming of the *peti* to synagogue worship once s/he has reached majority (twelve or thirteen years of age) and would count such a person in a minyan. On the other hand, he would not include a *shoteh* who might be diagnosed as severely mentally ill and truly unaware of or unable to relate to a worship service. Even so, such persons should be encouraged to join as much as possible in the life of the community, to the degree that they can do so without being disruptive to others or are themselves unhappy.[16]

5. Reform Perspectives

We should be sensitive to the fact that disabled persons, particularly the deaf, have traditionally been regarded in light of what they can *not* do, rather than considering positively the unique capabilities they have. We should encourage the inclusion of all disabled persons in our congregations and, where indicated, encourage the formation of special support groups.

Our *she'elah* asks whether the community or congregation has an express "obligation" in this respect. The answer is yes with regard to the principle. We deal here with a mitzvah and include it under the obligations we have with regard to our fellow human beings *(mitzvot bein adam l'chaveiro),* and the important part such mitzvot play in Reform Jewish life and theology.[17]

Of course, their application must be considered in the context of the congregation's and rabbi's resources. We cannot obligate any rabbi or congregation to provide special services to all disabled persons who come within their purview, but the obligation to be of whatever service possible has the status of a mitzvah. Without stating what is or what is not possible in a particular community, the following opportunities may serve as examples:

When we include the disabled in our *minyanim,* we must attempt to include them fully and facilitate their participation in the spiritual life of the community. For instance, large-

[15]BT *Chagigah,* 3b–4a. The discussion revolves around the question of whether any one of these acts is enough to characterize one as a *shoteh*. Sh. A., Yoreh De'ah 1:5 deems one of these actions sufficient.
[16]"The Difference Between 'Shoteh' and 'Peti' and the Obligation of Keeping Commandments and Learning Torah in Relation to a 'Peti,'" in *Behavioral Sciences and Mental Health,* Paul Kahn, special issue ed. (New York: Sepher Hermon Press, 1984), 229.
[17]See *Gates of Mitzvah,* Simeon J. Maslin, ed. (New York: CCAR, 1979), 97–115 for a discussion of the role of mitzvot in Reform Judaism.

print and Braille prayer books and texts, hearing aids, sign-language interpreters, and wheel-chair access to all parts of the synagogue building and sanctuary fall under the rubric of mitzvah and present the community with challenges and opportunities. New technologies will facilitate in-home electronic participation in services and classes. Sometimes, aesthetics and mitzvah may seem to clash: a ramp for wheel chair access to the pulpit may present a visual detraction, but it will also be inspiring for the congregation to know that its religious obligations toward the handicapped have been fulfilled. And obviously, where new buildings are constructed the needs of the disabled must be taken into consideration in the planning. As Reform Jews, we should allow for a creative interpretation of the mitzvot that would help to incorporate disabled persons into the congregation in every respect.[18]

In addition to providing physical facilities, we must provide the handicapped with the education that they will need to participate fully, or as fully as they can, in the life of the congregation. Where necessary, several congregations in the city should combine their resources to make this possible.

The aim of inclusion of the disabled is their complete participation in Jewish life. Therefore, we would, for instance, permit a blind student to read the Torah portion from a Braille Bible, if not from the Torah scroll itself though this would not constitute a halachically sanctioned reading, since it may not be done from memory.[19] We see the mitzvah of including the deaf as overriding the traditional prohibition.

A deaf bar/bat mitzvah student, depending on his/her capacity, could read from the Torah, or write a speech and have someone else deliver it, or deliver it in sign language him/herself and have an interpreter speak it to the congregation.[20]

Mentally disabled persons should be encouraged to do as much as possible.

---

[18]Rabbi Joseph Glaser recounts an example of such creativity: a deaf, and basically speechless, boy calligraphed his Torah portion, incorporating its theme (the burning bush) into the artwork (personal communication, 1991).

[19]BT *Gittin* 60b, Rambam, Hilkhot Tefillah 12:8, Sh.A., OH 53:14 and YD 139:3, cited in J. David Bleich, *Contemporary Halakhic Problems,* vol. 2 (New York, 1983), 30. Though the *Shulchan Aruch* rules that a blind person may not be called to the Torah, since one is not permitted to read it from memory (OH 139:3), this ruling is challenged by a number of authorities who hold that the obligation of the one called up to read the Torah portion personally no longer applies (Maharil, quoted by Isserles ad loc.; Mordechai Yaffe, Levush, OH 141:3; Bayit Chadash to Tur, OH 141; Magen Avraham, OH 139, n. 4; Turei Zahav, Orach Chayim 141, # 3; Mishnah Berurah, OH 139, #12). The Conservative Movement issued a responsum in 1964 regarding a blind man's wish to read the Torah for the congregation on Shabbat using Braille. The responsum, signed by Ben Zion Bokser, then chairman of the Committee on Jewish Law and Standards, states, "We would not regard it appropriate for a person to read the Torah from Braille. Such reading would have the same status as reading from the printed text of *Chumash,* which is not regarded as valid." However, a blind man may bless the reading of the Torah when it is read on his behalf by a reader. The bar mitzvah may, according to some authorities, recite the haftarah from memory or from a Braille text, while others require that a sighted reader repeat the haftarah prior to the final blessings over the reading by the bar mitzvah.

Mark Washofsky notes: "R. Binyamin Slonick, a student of R. Moshe Isserles in the sixteenth century, in Resp. Mas'at in Benyamin, # 62, addresses the question whether a blind person may be called to the Torah. In doing so, he remarks that he himself has become blind in his old age and that those such as R. Yosef Karo (Beit Yosef, OH 141) who prohibit this practice would 'expel me from God's portion, the Torah of Truth and eternal life.' His language testifies not only to his ultimate halachic conclusion that the blind are in fact permitted to be called to the Torah, but also to his fervent wish that the law not be otherwise. His is not an attitude of resignation, a passive readiness to accept whatever lot assigned to him by the Torah; he actively desires that halachah not exclude him from a ritual that has long been a source of much satisfaction to him." ("Some Notes on the Rights of the Disabled"; unpublished paper, 1991).

[20]Such a student might be reminded of Moses' speech impediment, which did not hinder him from becoming Judaism's greatest leader. He or she might also want to read Les Gruber's article, "Moses: His Speech Impediment and Behavior Therapy," *Journal of Psychology and Judaism* 10 (spring/summer 1986): 5–13. He takes Moses' description of himself as *k'vah peh u-khevad lashon* (Exodus 4:10) to mean that he stuttered and that the Torah account accurately describes the sort of therapy stutterers use today to overcome their disability.

Many of these issues are not only similar to, but directly concern, elderly individuals. Indeed, hearing, visual, mental, and physical disabilities often come as part of the aging process. Just as the Jewish community has gone out of its way to provide proper facilities for the aged, so should it make adequate resources available for the mentally and physically disabled of all ages. The fate of the tablets of the Decalogue describes our obligation: "The tablets and the broken fragments of the tablets were deposited in the Ark."[21] There was no separate ark for the broken tablets: they were kept together with the whole ones.

In sum, our worth as human beings is based not on what we can do but on the fact that we are created in God's image.[22] We should aim for the maximum inclusion of the disabled in the life of our communities.

Copyright © 2000, Central Conference of American Rabbis

---

[21]Numbers Rabbah, Bamidbar 4:20.
[22]M *Sanhedrin* 4:5, BT *Sanhedrin* 37A.

Caring for Those with Mental Illnesses

Resolution Adopted by the 108th Annual Convention of the Central Conference of American Rabbis June 1997

WHEREAS, the CCAR is deeply concerned for the physical, emotional, and spiritual well-being of every person in our society, and

WHEREAS, the millions of people who suffer from mental illness carry the added burden of being shunned, avoided, and stigmatized by many of their fellow citizens, and

WHEREAS, the direct cost to society for the treatment of mental illness and substance abuse comes to hundreds of billions of dollars, and

WHEREAS, acts of *chesed* including caring for the disabled are basic tenants of Judaism, as well as essential elements of any society, and

WHEREAS, the mitzvah of *hachnasat orchim,* welcoming others into our lives, calls on us to be particularly sensitive to the outcast and the scorned, and

WHEREAS, mental illness affects not only the individual but entire extended families, and

WHEREAS, the religious community has a clear responsibility to help create awareness and sensitivity in responding to mental illness and the mentally ill, and to help reduce the stigma that persons with mental illness and their loved ones experience, and

WHEREAS, most private health insurance policies discriminate against persons who suffer from severe mental illnesses by imposing lower lifetime limits, lower annual caps, higher deductibles, higher co-pays, and other limits on coverage that are not imposed for other diseases of the body,

THEREFORE BE IT RESOLVED, that the CCAR

1. calls upon its members to work with their congregations, chaplaincies, and other constituencies to inform them of the necessity for greater sensitivity with respect to the mentally ill and their needs, and to help reduce the stigma of mental illness, and

2. calls upon its members to participate in communal efforts aimed at providing a more positive attitude toward those suffering from mental illness, and

3. calls upon its members to work with persons afflicted with mental illness and their families so that they may feel welcome within our synagogues, as Abraham made strangers feel welcome in his home, and

4. calls upon its members to visit patients, when appropriate and professionally advisable, in psychiatric hospitals and other mental health-care facilities, and to join groups that seek to provide housing and employment for de-institutionalized persons, and

5. agrees to work with the Union of American Hebrew Congregations to establish a Joint Commission on Mental Illness, and

6. commends the work of the National Alliance for the Mentally Ill (NAMI) in Washington, and the work of Pathways to Promise: Interfaith Ministries and Prolonged Mental Illnesses, in St. Louis, and encourages our colleagues to be in touch with them, and

7. calls upon its members to support and advocate for federal and state legislation that protects against all forms of discrimination by health insurance carriers in the coverage of severe mental illnesses relative to other diseases of the body.

Resolution on Establishing a Complete System of Care for Persons with Mental Illnesses

Adopted by the Board of Trustees of the CCAR, June 2001

Mental illness can shatter lives. It is a condition often lacking explicit physical manifestations, and thus is both easily hidden and easily denied. Like physical illnesses, and perhaps even more so, the ramifications of mental illnesses are experienced in every sector of life. Whether or not people with mental illnesses receive treatment, such illness is therefore best considered not only as a medical issue, but also as an important social one with far-reaching economic and human welfare implications. Judaism concerns itself with the health and well-being of the mind and the soul as well as the body. Maimonides wrote: "When one is overpowered by imagination, prolonged meditation, and avoidance of social contact, which he never exhibited before, or when one avoids pleasant experiences, which were in him before, the physician should do nothing before he improves the soul by removing the extreme emotions."

Likewise, in the *mi shebeirach* prayer for the sick, we pray for a *r'fuah sh'leimah*—a complete recovery—and further specify *r'fuat hanefesh u'refuat haguf,* a healing of the soul and the body. Our tradition recognizes a distinction between mental and physical health, but treats them on an equal plane, recognizing that both are necessary for us to be complete.

In this context, we examine the issue of mental illness, and its multiple and far-reaching manifestations for individuals from all walks of life.

Adults

Mental illness strikes often, affecting millions of men, women, and children across North America, in both our communities and in our synagogues. Approximately 23 percent of

American and Canadian adults (ages eighteen and older) suffer from a diagnosable mental disorder at some point during their lives, but only half of those report impairment of their daily functioning due to the mental disorder. Of this number, approximately 5 percent are diagnosed as having a serious mental illness, such as schizophrenia, major depression, or bipolar disorder. In addition, 25 percent to 50 percent of all people with mental illnesses are believed to have a substance abuse disorder. While the definitions and terms are varied, we here refer both to those defined as having a diagnosable mental disorder and those with a serious mental illness, as well as those with co-occurring substance abuse disorders, when using the term "people with mental illnesses."

The Elderly

Almost 20 percent of the U.S. population age fifty-five and older experience specific mental illnesses that are not part of the "normal" aging process. The elderly population is also the demographic group within the United States most likely to commit suicide. We, thus, must seek to draw special attention to the elderly within our population who suffer from mental illness.

Children

Mental illness is also prevalent among children and teenagers within North America. Approximately 20 percent of children and adolescents, eleven million in all, are believed to have mental health problems that can be identified and treated. At least one in twenty children—three million in all—may have a serious emotional disturbance, defined as a mental health problem that severely disrupts a juvenile's ability to function socially, academically, and emotionally. Each year, almost five thousand young people, ages fifteen to twenty-four, commit suicide in this country. We will here refer to children with both mental health problems and serious emotional disturbances as "children with mental illness."

Parity

An important issue facing North America today is the lack of availability and access of individuals to mental health treatment, and the need for mental health insurance parity, defined as the requirement that health plans provide the same annual and lifetime limits for mental health benefits as they do for other health care benefits. The Reform Movement has consistently supported health care for all, declaring in 1975, for example: "In the United States there should be made available national comprehensive prepaid single-benefit standard health insurance with no deductible to cover prevention, treatment, and rehabilitation in all fields of health care." Currently, however, great inequities exist between coverage of mental health care and physical health care.

Employment and Mental Illness

According to a report by the Association for Health Services Research and the National Alliance for the Mentally Ill, employers bear significant costs due to mental disorders of their employees, probably more than they realize, because many costs are difficult to measure or are not easily recognizable as being caused by mental illness. Depression, for example, results in $30 billion a year in direct and indirect costs to employers. Depressed employees use 1.5 to 3.2 more sick days per month than other employees—lost time that costs employers $182 to $395 per worker per month, according to a study by the U.S. Centers for Disease Control and Prevention (CDC). Mental illness also takes many potential workers out of the labor force. Of disabled workers, more than 22 percent of those who receive Social Security Disability Insurance (SSDI) benefits and 30 percent of those who receive Social Security Insurance (SSI) qualify because of mental illness. Yet research has shown that people with mental illness have high productivity potential and that they can work and remain in the labor market for significant periods of time. It is thus vital to advocate for increased attention to ways in which persons with mental illnesses can continue to serve as productive members of the work force, and advocate for protections of these persons once in the workplace.

Homelessness and Mental Illness

According to the National Coalition for the Homeless, approximately 20–25 percent of the single adult homeless population in the United States suffer from some form of severe and persistent mental illness. In Canada, it is estimated that approximately one-third of the homeless in major Canadian cities suffer from a mental illness. The problems of homelessness and mental illness exacerbate each other. Mental illnesses, without proper treatment, prevent people from carrying out essential functions of daily life, thus pushing individuals out of mainstream society, out of jobs, and, ultimately, out of homes. Mental illness and lack of medical treatment also lead to the use of drugs and alcohol as forms of self-medication, increasing the inability of individuals to function within society. At the same time, homelessness prevents recovery or worsens mental illness; a mentally ill individual will often slip through the cracks of conventional programs and treatments, never obtaining the treatment and medication necessary to regain wellness. Many of these homeless, mentally ill individuals then end up in the criminal justice system, as discussed in the next section. According to the U.S. Department of Justice, mentally ill state prison inmates in the United States were more than twice as likely as other inmates to report living on the street or in a shelter in the twelve months prior to arrest (20 percent compared to 9 percent).

A shortage of affordable housing also exists, further challenging the ability of persons with mental illness to live off of the streets. Between 1973 and 1993, 2.2 million low-rent units disappeared from the market. These units were either abandoned, converted into condominiums or expensive apartments, or became unaffordable because of cost increases. Between 1991 and 1995, median rental costs paid by low-income renters rose 21 percent; at the same time, the number of low-income renters increased. A housing trend with a particularly severe impact on homeless persons with mental illnesses is the loss of single room occupancy (SRO) housing. In the past, SRO housing served to house many poor individuals, especially poor persons suffering from mental illness or substance abuse. From 1970 to the mid-1980s, an estimated one million SRO units were demolished.

Mental Illness and the Criminal Justice System

In addition, we must also be concerned where mental illness intersects adversely with the criminal and civil justice systems. In 1998, 283,800 people with mental illnesses were incarcerated in American prisons and jails. This is four times the number of people in state mental hospitals throughout the country. Sixteen percent (179,200) of state prison inmates, 7 percent (7,900) of federal inmates, 16 percent (96,700) of people in local jails, and 16 percent (547,800) of probationers have reported a mental illness. According to a 1999 U.S. Department of Justice study, approximately 53 percent of mentally ill inmates were in prison for a violent offense, compared to 46 percent of other inmates. While many believe that these mentally ill offenders must be held in jail because of the serious, violent nature of their offenses, it is vital that they receive treatment while incarcerated. We must be concerned, as well, with the civil liberties consequences of some forms of treatment for mental illness within the criminal justice system, especially the use of mechanical and physical restraints and the imposition of mandatory treatments. It is equally important that nonviolent offenders receive proper medical treatment, and that noncustodial treatment programs are explored and made accessible to offenders with mental illnesses, who are often turned away from community treatment because of a reluctance to treat them.

Further, while we have recently reaffirmed our opposition to the death penalty in all cases, we believe it to be especially unconscionable to execute the mentally ill even if the death penalty is otherwise to be imposed, and we will work to find common ground with supporters of the death penalty who oppose executing those with mental illnesses.

The prevalence of juveniles with mental illnesses within the juvenile justice system is astounding. Approximately 50–75 percent of youth in juvenile detention facilities suffer from mental illnesses, and approximately half of these youth with mental illness in the juvenile justice system suffer from co-occurring substance abuse disorders. Each year approximately 11,000 boys and 17,000 girls attempt to commit suicide while living within juvenile facilities. According to the Department of Justice's Office of Juvenile Justice and Delinquency Prevention, however, 75 percent of juvenile facilities do not meet basic suicide prevention guidelines, and many detention facility staff are never trained to recognize and respond appropriately to the symptoms of mental health disorders.

Coordinated Systems of Care

The absence of a coordinated system of care for individuals with mental illnesses has resulted in inefficient dispersal of responsibility for care and treatment of persons with mental illness. This is especially true for individuals with co-occurring substance abuse disorders, who are often turned away from mental illness treatment facilities. The United States government has begun to draw attention to the situation of the mentally ill in America today. In 1999, the president hosted the first White House Conference on Mental Health, calling for a national antistigma campaign. The surgeon general issued a Call to Action on Suicide Prevention in 1999, and the surgeon general's first Report on Mental Health was also issued in 1999. For decades, private and nonprofit organizations have worked tirelessly to establish access to services and protect the rights of persons with mental illness and to call for a holistic system of care for those who are in need.

Therefore, the Central Conference of American Rabbis resolves to:

1. call upon its member rabbis to:
   a. participate in communal efforts aimed at destigmatizing mental illness, and work with other members of the Jewish community to develop resources and programming aimed at addressing stigmatization of mental illness;
   b. work with persons afflicted with mental illness and their families so that they may feel welcome within our synagogues;
   c. prepare materials for training synagogue, religious school, camp, and youth program personnel to recognize and deal appropriately with members and participants with mental illnesses;
   d. work with other groups performing mental health outreach within the Jewish community toward persons with mental illness;
2. call for increased governmental and community support and development of programming for caregivers of those with mental illnesses;
3. call on the United States and Canadian governments to maintain and increase funding for federal programs aimed at treating those with mental illness and assisting them to live healthy and independent lives;
4. call on the United States and Canadian governments to increase funding for mental health research and the development and testing of innovative mental health programs, including those focusing on the co-occurrence of mental health disorders and substance abuse disorders;
5. encourage governmental integration and coordination of quality housing and mental health systems to provide comprehensive assistance, with special attention paid to the number of individuals with mental illness who live on our streets and in our shelters;
6. call for federal and state legislation to require parity between physical and mental health coverage by health insurance carriers, both private and public;
7. call for increased attention to the many inmates in our nation's prisons with mental illnesses, focusing on the need to:
   a. encourage the diversion of nonviolent, mentally ill criminal offenders into community-based mental health programs, and also work to ensure that individuals with mental illness sentenced to prison receive appropriate and humane treatment, including access to appropriate medication;
   b. call upon law enforcement agencies to develop policies, practices, and specialized training for police officers and corrections officers to recognize and deal appropriately with persons with mental illnesses;
   c. call for increased governmental attention to the youth within the justice system, and the need for increased funding for community-based treatment programs for mentally ill juvenile offenders;
   d. call on state and federal jurisdictions within the United States that retain the death penalty to exclude from consideration for the death penalty persons with mental illness;
   e. encourage an end to workplace discrimination against the mentally ill, and also encourage governmental development of further programs to assist those with mental illness in returning to the work place, and assist employers in working with them;
8. call for an increased focus on the mental health needs of children, including teenagers, by advocating for:

    a. the necessity of a coordinated system of care for children and teenagers with mental health problems;

    b. an emphasis on early recognition, prevention, and intervention, especially focusing on the prevention of suicide;

    c. increased research on the mental health problems of juveniles; and

    d. increased attention toward mental health needs within the schools and among professionals dealing with children in child care facilities and schools, as well as the development and implementation of training programs for these individuals;

9. call for increased focus on the recognition, prevention, intervention, and treatment of depression and other related mental illnesses in the elderly population.

Resolution on Establishing a Comprehensive System of Care for Persons with Mental Illness

Adopted by the UAHC
66th General Assembly
December 2001

While the definitions and terms are varied, we here refer to both persons defined as having diagnosable mental disorder and those with a serious mental illness, as well as those with co-occurring substance-abuse disorders, when using the term "persons with mental illnesses."

Mental illness can shatter lives. It is a condition often lacking explicit physical manifestations, and thus is both easily hidden and easily denied. Like physical illnesses, and perhaps even more so, mental illnesses and their ramifications are experienced in every sector of life. Treatment—or lack thereof—of persons with mental illnesses is therefore best considered not only as a medical issue, but also as an important social one with far-reaching economic and human welfare implications.

Judaism concerns itself with the health and well-being of the mind and the soul as well as the body. Maimonides wrote:

> When someone is overpowered by imagination, prolonged meditation and avoidance of social contact, which he never exhibited before, or when he avoids pleasant experiences which were in him before, the physician should do nothing before he improves the soul by removing the extreme emotions.

The reality is that mental illness continues to be stigmatized in our society. While people with physical illness are usually treated with solicitude and concern, persons with mental illness are frequently the objects of ridicule, contempt, or fear. While we often go to great lengths to accommodate and include people with physical illness, the mentally ill are frequently marginalized and excluded.

In this context, we examine the issue of mental illness, and its multiple and far-reaching manifestations for individuals from all walks of life.

Adults

Mental illness strikes often, affecting millions of men, women, and children across America, in both our communities and in our synagogues. Approximately 23 percent of American and Canadian adults (age eighteen and older) suffer from a diagnosable mental disorder at some point during their lives, but only half of those report impairment of their daily functioning due to the mental disorder. Of this number, approximately 5 percent are diagnosed as having a serious mental illness, such as schizophrenia, major depression, or bipolar disorder. In addition, 25 percent to 50 percent of all people with mental illnesses are believed to have a substance-abuse disorder.

Almost 20 percent of the U.S. population age fifty-five and older experiences specific mental illnesses that are not part of the normal aging process. This population is also the U.S. demographic group most likely to commit suicide.

Children

Mental illness is also prevalent among children and teenagers within North America. Approximately 20 percent of children and adolescents, 11 million in all, are believed to have mental health problems that can be identified and treated. At least one in twenty children— 3 million in all—may have a serious emotional disturbance, defined as a mental health problem that severely disrupts a juvenile's ability to function socially, academically, and emotionally. Each year, almost five thousand young people aged fifteen to twenty-four commit suicide in this country.

Parity

An important issue facing North America today is the lack of availability and access for individuals to mental health treatment, exacerbated by the need for mental health insurance parity, defined as the requirement that health plans provide the same annual and lifetime limits for mental health benefits as they do for other health care benefits. The UAHC has consistently supported health care for all, declaring in 1975, for example: "In the United States there should be made available national comprehensive prepaid single-benefit standard health insurance with no deductible to cover prevention, treatment, and rehabilitation in all fields of health care." Currently, however, great disparities exist between coverage of mental health care and physical health care.

Employment and Mental Illness

According to a report by the Association for Health Services Research and the National Alliance for the Mentally Ill, employers bear significant costs due to mental disorders of their employees, probably more than they realize, because many costs are difficult to measure or are not easily recognizable as being caused by mental illness. Depression, for example, results in $30 billion a year in direct and indirect costs to employers. Depressed employees use 1.5 to 3.2 more sick days per month than other employees—lost time that costs employers $182 to $395 per worker per month, according to a study by the U.S. Centers for Disease Control and Prevention (CDC). Mental illness also takes many potential workers out of the labor force. Of disabled workers, more than 22 percent of those who receive Social Security Disability Insurance (SSDI) benefits and 30 percent of those who receive Social Security Insurance (SSI) qualify because of mental illness. Yet research has shown that people with mental illness have high productivity potential and that they can work and remain in the labor market for significant periods of time. It is thus vital to advocate for increased attention to ways in which persons with mental illnesses can continue to serve as productive members of the work force and to advocate for protections of those persons once in the workplace.

Homelessness and Mental Illness

According to the National Coalition for the Homeless, approximately 20–25 percent of the single adult homeless population in the United States suffers from some form of severe and persistent mental illness. In Canada, it is estimated that approximately one third of the homeless in major Canadian cities suffer from a mental illness. The problems of homelessness and mental illness exacerbate each other. Mental illnesses, without proper treatment, prevent people from carrying out essential functions of daily life, thus pushing individuals out of mainstream society, out of jobs, and ultimately out of homes. Mental illness and lack of medical treatment also lead to the use of drugs and alcohol as forms of self-medication, increasing the inability of individuals to function within society. At the same time, homelessness prevents recovery or worsens mental illness; a mentally ill individual will often slip through the cracks of conventional programs and treatments, never obtaining the treatment and medication necessary to regain wellness. Many of these homeless, mentally ill individuals then end up in the criminal justice system, as discussed in the next section. According to the U.S. Department of Justice, mentally ill state-prison inmates in the United States were more than twice as likely as other inmates to report living on the street or in a shelter in the twelve months prior to arrest (20 percent compared to 9 percent).

A shortage of affordable housing also exists, compounding the problem. Between 1973 and 1993, 2.2 million low-rent units disappeared from the market. These units were either abandoned, converted into condominiums or expensive apartments, or became unaffordable because of cost increases. Between 1991 and 1995, median rental costs paid by low-income renters rose 21 percent at the same time, the number of low-income renters increased. In the past, Single Room Occupancy (SRO) housing served to house many poor individuals, especially poor persons suffering from mental illness or substance abuse. From 1970 to the mid-1980s, an estimated one million SRO units were demolished.

Mental Illness and the Criminal Justice System

An additional area of concern is the intersection between mental illness and the criminal and civil justice systems. In 1998, some 293,800 people with mental illnesses were incarcerated in American prisons and jails. This is four times the number of people in state mental hospitals throughout the country. Sixteen percent (179,200) of state-prison inmates, 7 percent (7,900) of federal inmates, 16 percent (96,700) of people in local jails, and 16 percent (547,800) of probationers have reported a mental illness. According to a 1999 U.S. Department of Justice study, approximately 53 percent of mentally ill inmates were in prison for a violent offense, compared to 46 percent of other inmates. While many believe that these mentally ill offenders must be held in jail because of the serious, violent nature of their offenses, it is vital that they receive treatment while incarcerated.

We must be concerned as well with the civil-liberties consequences of some forms of treatment for mental illness within the criminal justice system, especially the use of physical restraints and the imposition of mandatory treatments. It is equally important that nonviolent offenders receive proper medical treatment and that noncustodial treatment programs be explored and made accessible to offenders with mental illnesses, who are often turned away from community treatment programs because of reluctance to treat them.

Notwithstanding our existing policy of opposition to the dealth penalty in all circumstances, we take special note of the number of persons with mental illness who have been executed in the United States.

The prevalence of youth with mental illnesses within the juvenile system is astounding. Approximately 50–75 percent of those in juvenile detention facilities suffer from mental illnesses, and approximately half of these suffer from co-occurring substance-abuse disorders. Each year approximately 11,000 youths make 17,000 suicide attempts while living within juvenile facilities. According to the Department of Justice's Office of Juvenile Justice and Delinquency Prevention, however, 75 percent of juvenile facilities do not meet basic suicide-prevention guidelines, and many detention facility staff are never trained to recognize and respond appropriately to the symptoms of mental health disorders.

Coordinated Systems of Care

The absence of a coordinated system of care for individuals with mental illnesses has resulted in dangerous dispersal of responsibility for their care and treatment. This is especially true for individuals with co-occurring substance-abuse disorders, who are often turned away from mental illness treatment facilities. The U.S. government has begun to draw attention to the situation of the mentally ill in America today. In 1999, President Clinton hosted the first White House Conference on Mental Health, calling for a national campaign against stimatizing the mentally ill. The surgeon general issued a Call to Action on Suicide Prevention in 1999, and the surgeon general's first Report on Mental Health was also issued in 1999. For decades, private and nonprofit organizations have worked tirelessly to establish access to services, to protect the rights of persons with mental illness, and to call for a comprehensive system of care for those who are in need.

Caregivers

Currently, federal funding for 22 statewide family organizations is provided through the Child and Family Branch, Center for Mental Health Services, Substance Abuse and Mental Health Services Administration. Support and technical assistance are also provided by government agencies as well as by consumer groups via family support groups and respite-care services. An emphasis on the development of a coordinated system of care has also drawn attention to the needs of caregivers of individuals with mental illnesses. Over the past several decades, there has been a growing awareness of the difficulties families face because services are provided by so many different public and private sources. In addition to problems with coordination, parents and caregivers encounter conflicting requirements, different atmospheres and expectations, and contradictory messages from system to system, office to office, and provider to provider.

Therefore, the Union of American Hebrew Congregations resolves to:

1. prepare materials to be used for training synagogue, religious school, camp, and youth-program personnel to recognize and deal appropriately with members and participants with mental illnesses;
2. call upon all member congregations to:
   a. participate in communal efforts aimed at destigmatizing mental illness, and work with the entire Jewish community to develop resources and programming aimed at addressing stigmatization of mental illness;
   b. work with persons with mental illness and their families so that they may feel welcome within our synagogues;
   c. make use of the materials prepared by the UAHC to train personnel to recognize and deal appropriately with members and participants with mental illness; and
   d. work with other groups performing mental health outreach within the Jewish community toward persons with mental illness;
3. call for increased governmental and community support and development of programming for caregivers of persons with mental illnesses;
4. call on the U.S. and Canadian governments to maintain and increase funding for federal programs aimed at treating persons with mental illness and assisting them to live healthy and independent lives;
5. call on the U.S. and Canadian governments to increase funding for mental health research and the development and testing of innovative mental health programs, including those focusing on the co-occurrence of mental health disorders and substance-abuse disorders;
6. encourage governmental integration and coordination of quality housing and mental health systems to provide comprehensive assistance, with special attention paid to persons with mental illness who live on our streets and in our shelters;
7. call for federal and state legislation in the United States to require parity between physical and mental health coverage by health insurance carriers, both private and public, similar to the system of universal comprehensive mental health coverage in Canada;
8. call for state legislation in the United States to provide the necessary funding to fully implement the Olmstead Supreme Court decision to provide community based treatment for those persons with mental illness when such placement in a less restrictive setting is appropriate;
9. call on member congregations and the UAHC to provide health coverage for employees that guarantees parity in mental health coverage;
10. call for increased attention to the many inmates in our nations' prisons with mental illnesses, focusing on the need to:

    a. place nonviolent, mentally ill criminal offenders into community-based mental health programs, and also work to ensure that persons with mental illness sentenced to prison receive appropriate and humane treatment, including access to appropriate medication;

    b. limit the use of involuntary physical restraints and the imposition of mandatory treatment solely to instances that are not otherwise manageable;

    c. limit civil commitment and mandatory treatment to circumstances where it is used only with due-process protections;

    d. call upon law-enforcement agencies to develop policies, practices, and specialized training for police offices and corrections officers to recognize and deal appropriately with persons with mental illnesses;

    e. call for increased governmental attention to the youth within the justice system, and the need for increased funding for community-based treatment programs for mentally ill juvenile offenders;

    f. call on state and federal jurisdictions within the United States that retain the death penalty to exclude from consideration for the death penalty persons with mental illness; and

    g. work to find common ground with all groups—including those who otherwise support the death penalty—who oppose the execution of persons with mental illnesses;

11. encourage an end to workplace discrimination against persons with mental illness, in fact as well as in law, and also encourage governmental development of further programs to assist persons with mental illness in returning to the workplace, and to assist employers in working with them;

12. call for an increased focus on the mental-health needs of children, including teenagers, by advocating for:

    a. a coordinated system of care for children and teenagers with mental health problems;

    b. an emphasis on early recognition, prevention, and intervention, especially focusing on the prevention of suicide;

    c. increased research on the mental health problems of juveniles; and

    d. increased attention toward mental-health needs within the schools and among professionals dealing with children in child-care facilities and in schools, as well as toward the development and implementation of training programs for these individuals; and

13. call for increased focus on the recognition, prevention, intervention, and treatment of depression and other mental illnesses in the adult population.